TWIN

ALSO BY ALLEN SHAWN

Wish I Could Be There: Notes from a Phobic Life

Arnold Schoenberg's Journey

TWIN

A MEMOIR

ALLEN SHAWN

Viking

VIKING
Published by the Penguin Group

3 1712 01345 5228

Penguin Group (USA) Inc., 375 Hudson Street, New York, New York 10014, U.S.A. • Penguin Group (Canada), 90 Eglinton Avenue East, Suite 700, Toronto, Ontario, Canada M4P 2Y3 (a division of Pearson Penguin Canada Inc.) • Penguin Books Ltd, 80 Strand, London WC2R 0RL, England • Penguin Ireland, 25 St. Stephen's Green, Dublin 2, Ireland (a division of Penguin Books Ltd) • Penguin Books Australia Ltd, 250 Camberwell Road, Camberwell, Victoria 3124, Australia (a division of Pearson Australia Group Pty Ltd) • Penguin Books India Pvt Ltd, 11 Community Centre, Panchsheel Park, New Delhi – 110 017, India • Penguin Group (NZ), 67 Apollo Drive, Rosedale, North Shore 0632, New Zealand (a division of Pearson New Zealand Ltd) • Penguin Books (South Africa) (Pty) Ltd, 24 Sturdee Avenue, Rosebank, Johannesburg 2196, South Africa

Penguin Books Ltd, Registered Offices:
80 Strand, London WC2R 0RL, England

First published in 2011 by Viking Penguin,
a member of Penguin Group (USA) Inc.

10 9 8 7 6 5 4 3 2 1

A portion of this book appeared in *The New York Times Magazine* as "Family Meal."

Excerpt from "Ed è subito sera" from *Poesie* by Salvatore Quasimodo, (Arnoldo Mondadori Editore, Milan). © 1942 Arnoldo Mondadori Editore S.p.A., Milano. Translated by Piergiorgio Nicoletti. Used by permission of the publisher and the translator.

LIBRARY OF CONGRESS CATALOGING-IN-PUBLICATION DATA
Shawn, Allen.
Twin : a memoir / Allen Shawn.
p. cm.
ISBN 978-0-670-02237-3
1. Shawn, Allen. 2. Autism—Patients—Biography. 3. Schizoaffective disorders—Patients—Biography. 4. Twins—Biography. I. Title.
RC553.A88S53 2011
616.85'88200922—dc22
[B]   2010027898

Printed in the United States of America
Designed by Daniel Lagin

Penguin is committed to publishing works of quality and integrity. In that spirit, we are proud to offer this book to our readers; however, the story, the experiences, and the words, are the author's alone.

In memory of William and Cecille Shawn,
Bessie Fitzgerald Thomas, and Irene Anderson Archibald,
and to all those who have tried to understand and care for Mary

CONTENTS

1

LOST

don't like losing things. I keep a list of books I know I once had, and know I've read, that I have somehow misplaced; *The Magic Mountain*, Loren Eiseley's *The Star Thrower*, *The Complete Claudine* by Colette are on it, along with at least forty other titles. Even when I lose a pair of pants, a sense of vexation, a confusion, arises in me that seems out of all proportion to the loss, and if the pants are suddenly presented to me apologetically at the dry cleaners, I feel a strange giddiness, a tincture of the kind of joy displayed by reunited families in movies about Mormon heaven. It is strange that in this world in which everything is sooner or later lost, where losing is the only certainty, one gets attached to even the smallest things and wants to be able to say goodbye even to a pair of pants, rather than have it simply disappear. One wants to see a logic in disappearances and to know when one is losing things. Even if, in the end, we get to keep nothing.

When I was around ten years old I had a hamster named Sawdust who lived with me in my room. (I was a privileged child, lucky enough to have a room of my own.) Sawdust spent most of his time running excitedly on the little metal wheel inside his cage. He was named after the shavings that filled the retractable bottom of his rectangular glass dwelling, and when he wasn't running he was either sleeping in a clearing he made in the shavings, eating what looked like miniaturized trail mix from a small bowl, or drinking greedily from a metal spout attached to a bottle of water hanging on the cage's side. I got used to waking up each morning to the sound of Sawdust's creaking wheel and the sight, just beyond the foot of my bed, of his cheerfully furry form in motion, running forward without going anywhere.

Over Christmas vacation the year I had Sawdust, I came down with a flu that made me wake up in the middle of the night in sweat-soaked pajamas and sheets, with my teeth chattering. Day or night I could feel my head and eyes hurting and, behind my eyes, a strange sensation, as if hundreds of ants were crawling around in my brain. I could never be quite sure when I woke up what time of day it was, because a kind of fog had descended on me in my fever, which made me sleep most of the time. When I tried to leave my bed, I felt pressed down by what seemed to be a leaden weight, which made standing up feel as if I were on an ocean liner in bad weather. My head and my thoughts seemed to not quite belong to me. My body seemed a kind of fragile support for some burdensome, heavy throbbing ball sitting on top of it. Meanwhile "I" remained outside it all, dispassionately observing my own flimsy scaffolding trying to get up to go to the bathroom, wearing drenched flannel pajamas that gave off a decayed, fetid smell.

A few days passed in this confused state. I entered dreams that weren't dreams. A glass of sweetened orange juice sitting right next to me on a little table would seem very far away, and the idea of "juice" would occupy a kind of billboard in front of my forehead, which I contemplated for an immeasurably long time. The sensation of the coldness of the orange juice glass would enter my thoughts, hoping to usurp the place of sensible words or ideas. If my parents came to the door of my room to check in on me, the timbres of their voices would linger in the room for hours afterward, and their spoken consonants and vowels would continue murmuring in the moldings and corners of the ceiling, flitting from place to place on the walls like butterflies. During my fever, the normal order of my perceptions was disrupted. A pain would announce itself in the muscle between my thumb and forefinger, and I would become focused on it at the expense of everything else. My throat would begin to feel like an enormous, scratchy cave filled with woolen haystacks and would occupy my consciousness with a strange fierceness. Orderly thoughts would lie dormant down in my pinched, vaguely sickened stomach, like dead animals at the bottom of a well. During the period of my flu everything outside me was remote, and I was oblivious to the external world.

After a few days of this isolation, my eyes stopped hurting, the ants stopped crawling inside my head, I regained my interest in being read to by my brother, and I was seized with an appetite for lamb chops with mashed potatoes and green beans. While I stayed in bed recuperating, my parents had gone ahead with their plans for an adult party, which meant that the sounds of sophisticated voices, boisterous laughter, and clinking glasses wafted to my room from down the hall.

During the party my mother came to look in on me. I could hear her footsteps and the rustling sound her shoulderless red dress made as it grew louder and louder, changing to a sharper, higher pitch in the narrow hallway leading to my room. She gave me a bowl of applesauce with aspirin and sugar crushed in it, which was the way I took pills at that age. While I was eating this she told me that, sadly, two days earlier, Sawdust had died.

I looked over the foot of my bed and saw that Sawdust's cage was gone.

After my mother left the room, I couldn't stop crying. I cried off and on for many hours, picturing Sawdust's little feet scurrying on the metal wheel and his eager sucking on the water spout in the cage. There was an intensity to my sadness that went beyond grief over Sawdust. My pet's sudden death released a torrent of tears that had been stored within some swollen balloon inside me, and it was as if I was crying—with all the self-pity of childhood—not only about Sawdust, but about all the griefs and sad surprises I had already experienced.

I guess this just confirms once again that emotions are essentially physical forces, and if they seem to express themselves at the strangest moments, it is because, like physical forces, they must sooner or later emerge and will eventually succeed in finding a vulnerable link in the chain of your defenses. If the floodtide is dammed up, it will break into a million little rivulets, each seeking egress, and once an opening is found, all the waters will pour through it. You hold your tongue when your wife or husband does something unforgivable, and then, at a trivial moment, when your resistance is low, some tiny infraction—forgetting to pay a bill, or to remove the trash, or to telephone the child's school—causes your anger to burst, and you find yourself delivering one of those global, ad hominem attacks ("You have never for a moment thought of anyone but yourself!") that you later regret.

In the same way, I cried over Sawdust's death in a way I had never cried about my sister, and had never even known I wanted to.

Sometimes I wonder if Mary feels sick all the time, or feels that everything outside her is happening across an immense gulf. No, I remind myself, obviously one would need to be in a position to compare this state of mind to something else to experience it as "sickness" or as peculiar. But surely she must experience pain and suffering, because her way of communicating is so rarely understood. Books tell me that people with Mary's difficulties may be "blind" to other minds, that they may suffer from "mind blindness." While most people, no matter how egocentric, instinctively know that other people have their own independent thoughts and independent experiences, and most people eventually come to see themselves in a context of socially ever-widening concentric circles, with the experiences of the people they encounter in the foreground, and beyond them the experiences of whole societies, historical periods, and mankind generally, for Mary, at least according to some experts, life isn't like that. She needs others, sees them, and takes delight in them, but they exist only as they are in relation to herself.

If you are born blind, you simply live in a world in which seeing is something other people do. While you can be taught about "seeing," it will remain almost like a myth. At the same time, you will have other perceptions that sighted people will never understand. You will suffer from things that other people don't even notice, and you will also "see" where others are blind. From my readings about the mentally disabled I have begun to think that this is true for Mary in her kind of blindness, but I will never be able to confirm whether I am right.

Perhaps the closest I can come to understanding her inner life is when I am sick, or exhausted, or anxious, or exhilarated, or have taken a drug that changes what I hear and see and feel. Such moments at least suggest that there are different ways of perceiving and being.

I am looking at a picture of Mary at the age of roughly five, with her translucent skin, a prominent brow, a hint of the Asiatic in the shape of her deep brown eyes, a sensual mouth slightly parted, wearing a peaceful expression that somehow hovers between attentiveness and reflection. There is a hint of darkness beneath her eyes. With her cupped right hand she holds the pinkie of her extended left, as if putting a ring on it. Her hair has been braided and carefully brushed; one hair band is visible, as is her large and lovely right ear, which almost looks like a seashell. Her white dress is decorated with little applique flowers. The bucolic setting is in fact the Shakespeare Garden in Central Park, where our mother liked to take us as children.

Now another picture, taken roughly thirteen years later, this one of Mary and me. The setting is a small town in Delaware. It is summer and Mary is wearing a bright yellow sleeveless dress. The white flower on its pocket echoes the flowers on the dress she wore at five. Her hair is now short and held by a beret on her right side. Again she seems alert and actively cheerful, perhaps amused. She looks toward me with her eyes squinting, smiling, her cheeks lifted, her teeth showing. She could be laughing quietly or speaking. She wears plastic bracelets and a watch on her left arm and, again, raises her left hand, almost as if she is about to play the piano. We are turned toward each other, and I am holding her gingerly, delicately, with my right hand gently on her back, as if lightly supporting her, while my left arm is behind my own back. There are a pen and a glasses case in my shirt pocket.

That Mary is mentally retarded and, according to her current diagnosis, exhibits features both of autism and of schizo-affective disorder might surprise someone looking at these pictures for the first time. A kind of luminous beauty can be seen in the faces of autistic people when they are young. However, Mary's look of connectedness might still come as a surprise. In fact it seems to me that in the second picture my own expression is more guarded than hers, as if I am both looking and questioning, and not expecting clear answers to my questions. It is a bit like the expression of an anthropologist standing next to someone whose society they are studying, whose language they have only partly learned. What actually surprises me most in this photo, as in nearly all the pictures I have of the two of us, is the comfort and contentment I see in it. My memory of visits to see Mary in our teenage years is of an extreme self-consciousness and sense of detachment, as if I were viewing my own actions from outside. I remember the anxiety I felt before I saw her, and a sense of relief afterward, but not the contentment, the deep sense of relaxation when we were together.

I cannot judge whether or not a stranger could discern our relationship in the second photo. Are we friends? A young couple? Siblings? We are, in fact, fraternal twins. We were born five minutes apart, sixty years ago.

Mary disappeared from my daily life when we were eight years old, when my parents placed her in an institution for the mentally disabled, and as a reader of my previous book will know, it took me painfully long even to recognize that the event had left a kind of ocean of disquiet in me that manifested itself in panic attacks and a lifelong struggle with agoraphobia, and in my difficulties negotiating some aspects of public life, as well as in my reactions to trivial losses. Indeed, that it was so hard for me to openly disclose my own problems was partially due to my fear of the mental illness that Mary had exhibited, and which had led, or so it had seemed to me as a child, to her being "ostracized" from the family. I suppose that as her twin, it was doubly hard for me to know how and where to draw the boundary line between her nature and mine, between the inherent strangeness of being a person and the kind of strangeness that led to what I saw as banishment from normal human society. Yet I wasn't aware of any of this when I was growing up. It wasn't until I reached late middle age that I could even begin to acknowledge that being Mary's twin was a central fact, perhaps *the* central fact, of my life. All I did feel was a kind of blank place inside, where memories and feelings should have been.

I would say that my first reaction to thinking of myself as a twin, and as Mary's twin in particular, is surprise. Every time I remind myself that her birthday and mine are the same; or think about the parallels between her life at an institution and mine at the college where I teach and live; or when I hear her familiar voice on the phone—"HiAllenhowareyou?" a question she speaks as if it were a one-word assertion—I do a kind of double take. Our connection is instantly shunted into the distance, as if by some mental Doppler effect that gives an impression of simultaneous nearness and farness. As soon as I remember the fact that we are twins, I forget it. The sadness of the loss, and the sadness of the original situation—having a twin who will always remain largely indecipherable—surfaces in me only at odd moments, through reactions to other things, or in the music I feel impelled to write, music through which one senses that some bleak reality has been lived through and, to a degree, survived.

I therefore begin this book almost with a feeling of disbelief, and with no small reluctance. I never intended to be a writer, and certainly not a memoirist. I have written music since I was ten years old and have always thought of myself as a composer. That my last book, which began as a study of phobias grounded in my own experience of them, turned out to be at least 50 percent reminiscence came as a surprise to me and to my editors. Even more surprising was that Mary became its central character, as if at the center of my ungovernable anxiety when I am at a height or in open or closed spaces, or far from what I deem to be "safe" territory, were Mary's own furies and my reactions to them.

I notice even in photos of myself taken recently that I often seem to be tilting my head, as I am in the photo with Mary, as if I am leaving room for her, or as if she were leaning on me. I guess that the things that are most revealing about us, that are stamped on our gestures and facial tics and ways of speaking and of picking up objects, can telegraph meanings about which we remain ignorant. Perhaps my reluctance to write about Mary is not just due to shyness or scruples, or even just to the dread that has collected around this central fact of my life, but also to what, in writing about it, I may unknowingly reveal about myself.

As I studied to become a composer at college and later in France, attempting to learn how to structure my own nonverbal and essentially emotional means of communication, it never occurred to me that someday I would need to use words to describe, and therefore to begin to understand, the perplexing situation into which I had been born. Although my music often seemed to give voice to a grief belied by my relatively sunny personality, and frequently drew its ideas from contradictory influences, as if expressing a kind of twinship in its very materials, I did not often think of myself as a twin. As a young adult and later as a parent, struggling to find a way out of an internal prison—the phobias and psychological restrictions that plagued me—it rarely dawned on me that my singular experience was really a contrapuntal one, and that only when I confronted the sense of loss and the duality at the heart of my life would I begin to achieve some semblance of wholeness—or at least what Freud might have called "normal loneliness." Finally in my late middle age the contradictions I had carried within me that I had not been able to acknowledge or put into words demanded some kind of expression in a language my sister cannot use, and the result was my previous book, *Wish I Could Be There*.

The fact is that my own story and Mary's are, as it were, intertwined. If I cannot ever fathom how life seems to her, I can at least write down what I am certain about, something about my experience of being her twin, something about how our lives unfolded on parallel tracks, and about how people bear and express the imprints left on them by others.

2

JULY 2005

I am on a visit to see Mary in Delaware and have stopped in to see her psychiatrist. This should be a routine excursion, but in fact is not. It is the first time I have been to Briarcliff by myself. ("Briarcliff" is an invented name, as are the names of some individuals in this book whose privacy needs to be protected.) Up until my early twenties I saw my twin sister only on visits once or twice a year with my parents. After that it was only once a year, when she was brought up from Delaware for yearly birthday lunches. I had been discouraged for so long from developing an independent relationship with her that once I became an adult I made little effort to have one. Our physical separation was made practically complete by my agoraphobia, which prevented me from making the trip down to see her. But after my father died and my mother's age began to show its effects, my brother and I had taken responsibility for Mary, and I finally found a way to get to Delaware myself and spend time with her there, where she has lived for more than forty years. This began a slow process of reconnecting with her.

When my brother and I were clearing out my mother's apartment, I found a number of old documents about Mary tucked away in bureau drawers. Notes from Mary's first evaluations at Briarcliff included these observations about my parents, that they were probably not meant to see:

> Father is a rather short, very anxious man, who is editor of the New Yorker Magazine. Mother is also a very anxious woman. Both parents seemed quite reluctant to convey any information about the nature of their anxiety or its cause.... Family Situation and Relationships: As indicated above, this is unclear, except that the two parents seems [sic] to be exceptionally anxious people, and I have the sense of some sort of mutual protective alliance underway. I could not discern the basis for this, or be sure who was protecting whom. I asked Mrs. Shawn if she might visit alone, as she put their inability to visit on Mr. Shawn's schedule, and she said that she had found it impossible to do this for reasons she would not go into.

My father, William Shawn, became editor of the *New Yorker* when Mary and I were only four years old. During my childhood he was under a lot of pressure at work and as a result of his highly sensitive and vulnerable constitution. As I do now, he suffered from phobias that severely curtailed his activities. Although he was highly secretive, these private torments became among the few well-known facts about his personal life, in part because they had public consequences, such as that he avoided occasions where large groups of people were gathered, and that the magazine kept a manually operated elevator in service because he preferred it to the automated kind. After his death, the fact that he had had a decades-long love relationship with a woman writer at the magazine also became well known, adding to the irony that someone as shy, tactful, and circumspect as he was had a public reputation not only for being an admired editor, but for aspects of his most private behavior. Whoever took those notes at Briarcliff was not wrong about my parents' anxieties. The trips to see Mary were very difficult, in different ways, for each of them.

The question of whether Mary's condition was the result of the way our parents treated her, or was somehow connected to their personalities, hovered at least vaguely over all the documents pertaining to Mary from the beginning, and it surely hovered over them as well. Whatever the strains may have been on their marriage, my parents still loved each other, and were loving and gentle to their children. It must have been baffling and chilling to be faced with a child who, for unknown reasons, in that age before "autism" was even partially understood, did not respond to them in a normal way.

When she was still a child, who could be absolutely certain what Mary's problems were, when and why they began, and if they were curable? At the age of two, how could one make the distinction between mental retardation and delayed intellectual development? How could one make a distinction between emotional trauma and an inborn disorder of the brain?

Sitting in Dr. Trombly's office, I don't feel that I am there only to discuss my sister. Inevitably, my own life, my brother's life, and my parents' lives are the subject as well. There is a strange irony to the fact that I am there at least in part because in writing a book about my phobias I have written more about Mary than I ever expected to, and that it is this that has made me push against the barriers of my nature and finally get to Briarcliff. I briefly bring Dr.

Trombly up-to-date on my progress with the book and with the changes in my life. I tell him about my children, Annie and Harold, and that Annie is now twenty-one, finishing college and hoping to go to graduate school to eventually become a psychologist. Harold is flourishing in high school. I tell him that I intend to remarry. I tell him about my composing projects and the classes I am currently teaching at Bennington. Since he is a music lover, I promise to send him some of my CDs. We also talk briefly about my brother, Wallace Shawn, who is a well-known playwright and actor.

Dr. Trombly is a tall, fastidious-looking man with a trim grey beard. In his simple grey suit and blue tie, chosen as if to be deliberately unobtrusive, he looks reassuring and exactly like what he is—a medical professional and professor. But he has a surprisingly warm, light, and even gently anarchic air about him as soon as he starts talking about his clients at Briarcliff. One senses immediately that he is on their side.

As I speak with Dr. Trombly about Mary, I am still struggling in my own way to grasp the meaning of the terms used in her diagnosis and to understand the difference between her being "retarded" as I used to understand her to be, and being labeled "mildly retarded with features of autism and schizo-affective disorder," as her diagnosis now describes her. I also struggle to determine in my own mind where I, as her twin, fit into the picture. I dimly remember her being referred to as autistic very early on, when we were no more than six years old, during the period when Bruno Bettelheim's first books about the treatment of emotionally disturbed children were being published. This designation was supplanted for many years simply by the blanket diagnosis of "brain damage" associated with mental retardation. During this visit, Dr. Trombly tries to allay my lifelong guilt about Mary's "brain damage," suggesting that the evidence now conclusively shows that most forms of autism are genetic in origin and not the result of birth trauma or of events occurring after birth. He tells me that Mary's nature was not suddenly impaired by her violent entrance into the world—a violence in which I was an infant participant—but was most probably formed from within, as she herself was forming.

But is she truly "autistic," I ask? (Inwardly I bridle at putting Mary in a category. To me, she is simply herself.) Trombly briskly outlines the essential features of autism but encourages me to read further in several new books on the subject, along with writings by Lorna Wing, who has studied autism's genetic underpinnings.

"I view autism as a broad heterogeneous category," he says, "with all the colors of the spectrum. I think that people are misled by the idea, commonly presented in the press, that autism is a single disorder whose cause must urgently be discovered. Autism consists of many disorders with many different causes. It is one of two major developmental disorders of childhood. The other is mental retardation (now called intellectual disability), which is generally accepted as including many conditions and resulting from many causes. Autism needs to be understood in the same way, and the concept of the autism spectrum disorders facilitates this understanding.

"Classic autistic disorder (Kanner syndrome) is characterized by three things: an absence or severe deficiency in speech, in which true communication is often replaced by mechanically repeated phrases (echolalia); a lack of connection to—or impulse to communicate with—other human beings, which at its most extreme can take the form of complete obliviousness to them; and a narrow range of interests and preoccupations (about which the autistic person often has an extraordinarily detailed knowledge and memory), coupled with a need for consistency and sameness in routine and environment.

"Put simply, the essential characteristics of classical autistic disorder are difficulties with communication and in the social sphere; repetitive or ritualistic behaviors; and narrow interests," he says. "These characteristics are present by the third year, but sometimes aren't apparent until then. About one-third of autistic children actually seem normal until age two and then regress—losing whatever speech they had acquired and losing their ability to socially interact with others. Though, of course, if we look back at home movies of these children later, we sometimes do see signs that went unnoticed at the time suggesting that they were autistic."

Later, back home in Vermont, I begin to read. Even getting my bearings in the readings is at first difficult. The primitive notion that when "something is wrong" with a person, that "something" is a discrete condition that can be simply diagnosed by physicians, traced to its origins, and treated is hard to shake. That each person's brain—whether he or she is deemed in the "healthy" range or not—is its own unique immensely complex entity may be an easy concept to grasp but collides with our need for simple explanations. Mary's condition was described differently at different times in her life. Furthermore, she exhibits aspects of different underlying problems, with autism as only one aspect. She is also "intellectually disabled," a condition that sometimes overlaps with autism, and at other times does not. Some documents pertaining to her say she also exhibits signs of schizo-affective disorder.

The meaning of the term "autism" has itself dramatically changed during my lifetime, and the idea of an autistic disorders "spectrum" is only thirty years old. It takes me a while to recognize the obvious fact that since the diagnosis is a recent one, it might seem as if there are more people with the condition than there used to be. The symptoms exhibited by those on the spectrum are, in the words of author Roy Grinker, "probably as old as humanity." It helps to be reminded by Uta Frith, in her authoritative book *Autism: Explaining the Enigma*, that many figures familiar from history and legend might well be diagnosed as having "classic autistic disorder" were they alive today. She makes the case that many of the accounts of the holy fools venerated in Russia from the Middle Ages all the way through the nineteenth century suggest that they often exhibited features of autism. She cites as an example the obsessive, repetitive behavior of the nineteenth-century "blessed fool" Pelagija Serebrenikova, who for many years, day after day, would "collect loose bricks and stones, carry them to a flooded pit, and throw them in one by one," and then "immerse herself in the water and pull out and toss back the stones she had thrown in." Apparently the very characteristics that could have made them the subject to abuse—their isolation, muteness, and freedom from social constraints—made them, in this case, the object of veneration. Similarly, she suggests that the legendary twelfth-century Franciscan monk famous for his selfless innocence, Brother Juniper, who was a follower of Saint Francis, was autistic. In the eighteenth century, the era of Jean Itard's *Mémoire et rapport sur Victor de l'Aveyron*, which in 1970 François Truffaut made into the unforgettable film *L'enfant sauvage (The Wild Child)*, some of those we would now consider autistic were believed to be "feral" or "wild."

The term "autism," from the Greek word αύτό (*autos*), meaning "self," only entered psychological terminology in 1911, introduced by the Swiss psychiatrist Eugen Bleuler in the context of his discussions of schizophrenia (a term he also invented). Autism literally means "selfism." Bleuler invented the term "schizophrenic autism" to describe the behavior of schizophrenics who seemed lost in their own thoughts, cut off from life, those exhibiting an almost wholesale "neglect of reality," who ceased to "care about the real world," those whose "actions and . . . whole attitude to life are insufficiently externally motivated."

I read about how, a generation after Bleuler, the child psychiatrist Leo Kanner used the term "autism" to describe a group of eleven children, ranging in ages from two to ten, whom he studied over a period of several years. Despite being of average or above-average intelligence, these children did not socially interact with others, instead exhibiting an "extreme autistic aloneness." Although some of the children referred to in his study had previously been diagnosed as schizophrenic, in Kanner's view they deserved a distinctly different diagnosis, first because schizophrenia tends to surface in early adulthood, as opposed to childhood, and second because there was no sign that they were experiencing hallucinations or suffering from delusions, as schizophrenics do. They were not "psychotic." In every case the children's extreme detachment from the social world had become apparent in their first months. As a result, he referred to them as suffering from "early infantile autism." In addition he found that these children "hated changes in routine, in the arrangement of furniture, or even in the path taken from one place to another." They were exceptionally sensitive to the patterns in their environments and lives, and they wanted these patterns to be unchanging.

A parallel study by the Austrian pediatrician Hans Asperger, who never met Leo Kanner but like Kanner used the word "autistic" to describe the characteristics of the children he studied, was written in 1944. Asperger's group of children, while sharing with

Kanner's subjects a marked impairment in their understanding of others and an inability to interact socially, tended to have a highly developed sense of language, beginning at a normal age. Many of these individuals would grow up to become highly successful, particularly in mathematical and scientific pursuits, while suffering limitations in the social sphere.

Originally the primary distinction between the two conditions seemed to be the early development of language in people with Asperger's. The commonalities between them were difficulties understanding and identifying with others, and the appearance of a narrow range of obsessive interests. It was the English social psychologist Dr. Lorna Wing, whose own daughter is autistic, who posited in a 1981 article in *Psychological Medicine* that what we now call "Asperger's syndrome" is in fact a form of high-functioning autism. Wing argued convincingly that the two conditions—those identified by Kanner and Asperger—should properly be seen as part of a continuum, a "spectrum" of "autistic disorders." (Among the strong pieces of evidence for this view are the cases of twins or triplets who share autistic features to varying degrees.) Thus many professionals now refer to "autism spectrum disorders," with "classical autism" (or "Kanner's autism") at one end of the spectrum and Asperger's syndrome at the opposite end. To Wing and most other experts in the field, this spectrum results from abnormalities in the brain, which are in turn the result of multiple genetic defects. According to Wing, as much as 1 percent of the population can locate itself on this spectrum.

However, there are experts in the field who feel that the diagnosis of Asperger's is now too routinely made and should be limited strictly to those for whom it causes significant suffering and for whom some form of treatment is essential. Still others argue that classic autism and Asperger's syndrome should be viewed not as extremes on a continuum but as different conditions.

At that first meeting Trombly mentioned to me that some people in the field could be faulted, in his view, for spreading the diagnosis of autism over too broad a segment of the population. "I was once at a meeting on Asperger's syndrome where a psychiatrist in the audience asserted that twenty percent of his classmates at MIT had Asperger's. No! No! No!" he said, laughing. "But it is appropriate to use the term 'autism' in connection with all conditions that meet the general criteria of impaired social communication and restrictive behaviors and interests.

"The degree of specificity of these interests in autistic young people can be quite startling," he continued, "and of course they can have the excellent memories to match. I knew a boy who was uniquely fascinated by Native American tribes and couldn't stop reading about them and talking about them. And another who was preoccupied with maps of train, trolley, and subway routes and timetables. In fact, he once boarded a trolley when no one was looking and drove it on its normal route until he was stopped by having a minor accident (in which, fortunately, no one was hurt). Needless to say, he knew everything about how the trolleys worked, what the trolley regulations were, the numbers on all the trolley cars, and all of their routes through the city."

He told me that one can be autistic with a high IQ or, as in Mary's case, autistic with impaired intellectual capacities. We also talked about the hair-trigger reactions of autistic people, their extraordinary sensitivities.

"They can have a hypersensitivity to many things," he said, "hypersensitive smell, a hypersensitivity to food, and extreme auditory sensitivities that make certain sounds truly noxious. You will be with someone in the shopping mall and they will become terribly upset by the noise, the multiplicity of different sounds. It will be unbearable for them. . . . Or they will walk into a room and hear a vacuum cleaner and hold their ears and scream, as if in pain.

"I wish we knew more," he said with a sigh when I asked him about the different "treatments" that today's parents of autistic children hear described. "On the one hand, it isn't fair to parents not to lay out the various therapy options that are out there, but on the other, one needs to be frank about the true range of possible outcomes. These children have such different trajectories. Given language therapy, for instance, some get better, and others simply get worse. Yet at a certain stage, these children look virtually the same. How they will do when given a certain treatment is unpredictable."

The very first dictionary definition of autism I find, in the *Concise Oxford English Dictionary*, is: "morbid absorption in fantasy." This suggests to me that, to a degree, we all have an autistic side. I can't help wondering if my own experience of "autistic aloneness" is in the protected, hypnotic state I seem to enter when I am composing music. Later I find this position—that autism, of a kind, is a part of everyone's psychology—expressed by the psychiatrist and psychoanalytic theoretician Thomas H. Ogden in his book *The Primitive Edge of Experience*.

I read Temple Grandin's *Emergence: Labeled Autistic* and *Thinking in Pictures*; Gunilla Gerland's *A Real Person*; Simon Baron-Cohen's *Autism and Asperger Syndrome: The Facts* and *Mindblindness*; Roy Grinker's *Unstrange Minds*; Uta Frith's *Autism and Asperger Syndrome*. Eventually it becomes impossible for me to relate all these varied readings to the Mary I know and the

Mary I grew up alongside. I can't take it all in, and I can't synthesize the information. I find myself rejecting the books, even rejecting the idea that there is anything *wrong* with Mary.

It is not until I read Kanner's eleven original case studies, in his 1943 article "Autistic Disturbances of Affective Contact," that I have a shock of recognition. Naturally, Mary does not resemble each person described here in every detail. And each of Kanner's case studies differs to some degree from the others—each person is individual. But there is a pattern, and it has something to do with social isolation, with an inability to communicate with and understand others. Mary's behavior, which was so highly unusual in the context of 1150 Fifth Avenue in Manhattan, here finds a general context in which she is part of a kind of norm.

Leo Kanner, who, like Hans Asperger, Bruno Bettelheim, and the young doctor who first studied Mary, Herta Wertheim, was an Austrian refugee and was working as director of Johns Hopkins University Hospital in Baltimore when he did his pioneering studies. A child of Orthodox Jews, he had been born in the tiny town of Klekotow in the Ukraine and spent his teenage years in Berlin, where he excelled in science and was the only Jew in a non-Jewish high school. Later he attended medical school at the University of Berlin. At the age of twenty-four, with a medical degree but no experience as a practicing psychiatrist, he had had the foresight to immigrate to America. (Several of his family members remained in Europe and perished in concentration camps.)

Kanner's observations of "autistic" personality traits began at home. His father and grandparents were, by his own account, emotionally inexpressive and flat; he even called them "paradigms rather than real people of flesh and blood." His father had the type of gift sometimes associated with those on the autistic spectrum, a phenomenal, near-photographic memory for texts and faces. Kanner seems to have inherited this gift, along with something of his father's social awkwardness.

Kanner's study of eleven disturbed children, whom he described as suffering from an "inborn autistic disturbance of affective contact," convinced him that their inability to connect with—or perhaps even comprehend the reality of—other human beings did not constitute the gradual psychological "withdrawal" from the social world associated with schizophrenia, but rather stemmed from an innate social disability. These children had "come into the world with an . . . inability to form the usual, biologically provided affective contact with people, just as other children come into the world with innate physical or intellectual handicaps."

Both startling and somehow familiar to me in Kanner's accounts are the testimonies of parents telling how they try to cope with what seem like bizarre behaviors, or the absence of expected behaviors, in their developing children. In retrospect, the parents tell how they realize that the absence of communication began long before speech or even smiling were to be expected. In Kanner's accounts mothers remember their surprise as they realized that their six-month- or year-old infants never reacted physically when they were about to be lifted up, but instead remained completely limp. (Even four-month-old infants tense their facial muscles and make a shrugging motion with their shoulders when they sense they are going to be picked up.) Nor did they make a baby's customary subtle bodily adjustments to being held. They seemed in fact not to *care* that they were being held. Eventually the parents realized that it was actually extremely difficult to get their child's attention at all, and still later that, in fact, any communicative interaction of any kind with the child was rare. By the time their child was three years old the parents would report to Kanner such things as:

He does not observe the fact that anyone comes and goes.

He doesn't want me to touch him or put my arm around him.

He walks as if he is in a shadow, lives in a world of his own where he cannot be reached.

His entire conversation is a replica of whatever has been said to him.

He is detached from the rest of the children, except when he is in the assembly; but if there is music, he will go to the front row and sing.

He has never asked a question nor answered a question.

Mostly she is quiet, as she has always worked and played alone.

She has no relation to children. . . . She moves among them like a strange being, as one moves between the pieces of furniture in a room.

Noting that some of the children brought to him had been de- scribed as either "feeble-minded" or schizophrenic, Kanner coun- tered that, taken together, the children manifested a number of common characteristics that suggest a "unique 'syndrome' not heretofore reported," which was distinct from schizophrenia and was not necessarily accompanied by low IQ. The "fundamental disorder is the children's *inability to relate themselves* in the ordi- nary way to people and situations from the beginning of life," he wrote. "There is from the start an *extreme autistic aloneness.*" Because they were so difficult to communicate with, many of the children Kanner studied had been at one time considered deaf. But Kanner interpreted their obliviousness to what was being asked of them or said to them as "an all-powerful need for being left undisturbed," an urgent need to continue a private repetitive routine. "Everything that is brought to the child from outside, everything that changes his external or even internal environment, represents a dreaded intrusion." Such intrusions could include food, "loud noises and moving objects," changes in the arrangement of furniture, of an expected pattern in a design, or the interruption of a daily schedule.

In this respect, Kanner argued, these children differed profoundly from schizophrenics. Whereas a schizophrenic knows what it is to be in touch with the world and willfully abandons it, these children as they age actually gradually move a bit toward the world—for instance, respond to "questions" and "commands" directed at them—"the sooner to be able to return to the still much desired aloneness."

The parents recounted how their children craved a life of repetition. "He almost never says a sentence without repeating it. Yesterday, when looking at a picture, he said many times, 'Some cows standing in the water.' We counted fifty repetitions, then he stopped after several more and then began over and over." The children insisted that objects and people in their world maintain their exact accustomed place in an ordered hierarchy: "He is upset when the sun sets. He is upset because the moon does not always appear in the sky at night." And although they seemed to never show signs of empathy for other children, they sometimes identified with inanimate things: "He frets when the bread is put in the oven to be made into toast, and is afraid it will get burned and be hurt." By contrast, people were sometimes viewed as if they were objects: "[S]he soon learned the names of all the children, knew the color of their eyes, the bed in which each slept, and many other details about them, but never entered into any relationship with them." "He never looked at anyone's face," and if anyone grabbed or stepped on an object he was playing with, he "became angry with the hand or the foot, which was dealt with per se and not as a part of a person."

In keeping with Asperger's patients, Kanner's subjects uniformly had difficulties with pronouns. It was almost as if they could not comprehend the need for them. Since language is learned by imitation, these children simply copied the pronouns they heard. When they wanted something, they referred to themselves in the third person ("Mary wants a cookie"). When they hurt themselves, they mimicked the warnings they had heard, and referred to themselves in the second person ("You'll get hurt").

I had mentioned to Trombly that I was rereading Bettelheim. In the 1950 and '60s, Bettelheim and some other experts in childhood mental illness naturally focused on the possibility of a cure and generalized from those who could be brought out of their social withdrawal that autism was not innate, but was a response to trauma and to parental, particularly maternal, rejection. When Mary's first examining doctors pronounced the word "autistic," it could have suggested to my parents that she was mentally traumatized, as were some of Bettelheim's patients who exhibited similar "autistic" tendencies.

"Yes, that is the old 'refrigerator mother' idea," Trombly had said. "But what would Bettelheim say about twins, when one becomes autistic and the other develops normally? He would have to say that the same mother at the same moment in her life was cold and rejecting to one child, to the extent of communicating a desire that the child cease to exist, while being warm and nurturing to that child's twin. This might happen very, very rarely, in some bizarre cases, but seems highly unlikely, to say the least."

Our father published several of Bettelheim's works in full or excerpted form in the *New Yorker*. Among these were the essays that became *The Uses of Enchantment*. Bettelheim also famously came to the defense of Hannah Arendt's *Eichmann in Jerusalem*, which was also published in the *New Yorker*. Therefore his name surfaced frequently in family conversations. His views about autism, when I first became aware of them, made me confused about the causes of Mary's condition.

I remember looking for a long time at the cover of Bettelheim's *The Empty Fortress* when I was a teenager, thinking that the book contained the answers to the mystery of what was wrong with Mary. The image of a small girl cradling a doll, lost in thought while smoothing the doll's hair, fascinated me. On the cover, the girl is wearing a dark dress with a collar outlined in little metal beads. With her left hand she is holding the doll close to her, covering the doll's mouth but leaving its wide, staring eyes exposed. By contrast, she herself is looking down, her eyes in shadow but suggesting deep concentration, as her palm gently caresses the doll's hair. On the one hand, it is as if the girl were a doctor and the doll her silent, unfathomable patient. On the other hand, the doll could be the girl's hidden, silenced self.

Bettelheim's first writings were eloquent essays on the psychological impact of surviving life in the concentration camps (he had spent a year as a prisoner in Dachau and Buchenwald), in which he drew parallels and noted distinctions between "concentration camp survivor syndrome"—an inability to "reintegrate" oneself after enduring the extreme suffering and imminent threat of death experienced in the camps—and psychosis experienced in more normal life circumstances:

> The psychotic person breaks because he has invested significant figures in his environment with the power to destroy him and his integration. . . . [While] the psychotic person only delusionally believes that there are all-powerful figures who control his life and who plan to destroy him, the concentration camp prisoner observed correctly that those in whose absolute power he was actually had destroyed others like him, and were bent on destroying him, too.

Bettelheim found his vocation in 1950s Chicago working with severely disturbed children—many of whom exhibited the features of what was then called "infantile autism"—as head of the Orthogenic School at the University of Chicago. As Bertram Cohler, a former patient at the school who eventually became a psychology professor at the university, put it, Bettelheim made the school into a kind of mirror image of the camps.

Bettelheim's approach to treatment was based on the assumption that the extreme violence, withdrawal, or self-destructiveness of these children was their "logical" reaction to an environment that they viewed as threatening their very existence. According to Cohler, the goal of the school was to take children who had been deemed incurable, children "no one could stand," and place them in an environment in which they felt cared for and safe. The staff's job was to find nonthreatening ways to contain their rage, rebelliousness, and self-destructiveness until, but by bit, they relaxed their grip on the patterns of behavior—which ranged from inspiring fear in others to extremes of silent self-deprivation, such as anorexia, the refusal to defecate, and so on—that stemmed from their original environment. Since these children had learned to mistrust adults, the building itself was designed to inspire these feelings of safety even before the staff could. Each child had his own space, which was viewed as inviolable—his own bed, his own possessions. Doors were not locked. Even the front door could lock only from the inside. If a child ran away, he was gently followed, but not pursued in a manner that would make him feel threatened. When a child was a danger to himself or others, ingenious methods were devised to protect against his behavior, without, for the most part, doing violence to him. For example, when a child routinely threw heavy furniture at others, the staff secretly bolted the furniture down, so that he would learn that it was possible for them to control the harmful effects of his actions without physically restraining him.

Bettelheim chronicled his work with autistic children in several book-length accounts, culminating in *The Empty Fortress* of 1967. Even the title, *The Empty Fortress: Infantile Autism and the Birth of Self,* communicates Bettelheim's essentially psychological interpretation of the condition. And in his introduction he makes explicit his personal connection to the state he found these children in, with all that this implies: "Some victims of the concentration camps had lost their humanity in response to extreme situations. Autistic children withdraw from the world before their humanity ever really develops." The book makes clear the author's belief that while an underlying medical cause for infantile autism might someday be determined, in his view "the precipitating factor in infantile autism is the parent's wish that his child should not exist.

While the same wish may not cause the same disturbance in other children, and while at some future time we may learn that some organic factor is a precondition of autism, the fact is that almost all organic conditions that have so far been linked to this disease are also present in non-autistic children." At the same time he posited the view that the parents' response to the behavior of autistic individuals in effect punishes them further for the difficulties they cause the family.

His books on the subject suggest that the school had an impressive success rate, with "eight in our forty for whom the end results of therapy were 'poor' because, despite improvement, they failed to make the limited social adjustment needed for maintaining themselves in society. For fifteen the outcome was 'fair' and for seventeen 'good.'" He goes on to say, "Some of the fifteen whom we classify as 'fair,' while completely able to feel in a two-way relation, show a capacity for empathy that is less than normal. . . . They are not responsive where the feelings of others do not pertain to themselves."

Bettelheim concludes that if those trained in his methods intervene early enough, they can reverse the course of what is essentially an emotional disturbance in the early development of a potentially more normal human being: "These findings, incidentally, suggest again that in infantile autism we are not dealing with an inborn disturbance of affective contact, but rather with an inborn time schedule that cannot be delayed for too long."

I heard of Bettelheim's Orthogenic School as a teenager (the word "orthogenic" means "straight growth") and often had the fantasy that Mary would be able to go there and be cured. I remember our father admitting that he had had the same fantasy. But I don't know whether he or our mother ever actually spoke to

Bettelheim about Mary, much less suggested a consultation. Bettelheim was referred to reverentially in the household. In those days in our family conversations people of such heroic stature were moral touchstones, almost as if they had transcended being merely human and had become platonic forms of themselves, abstractions: such people—W. H. Auden, Dag Hammarskjöld, Bruno Bettelheim himself, even the television journalist Eric Sevareid—were idealized as ethically beyond reproach, incapable of mixed motives or venality; in short, virtually flawless. Such people—so went the unspoken family view—might make "mistakes" but could be relied upon for the best of motives at all times. By implication, somehow it was understood that our father fitted into this category himself—despite his obvious weaknesses and complexities (some of which still remained hidden from us). And just as in the *New Yorker*, when great figures were written about, somehow the unpleasant, disorderly, dysfunctional, or destructive aspects of their humanity disappeared, in the same way our father's true complexity and the conflicts in his nature and daily routine were subjected to a kind of censorship at home.

Until the more negative accounts of Bettelheim's work and personality began appearing in the years immediately following his death, I had thought of him as similarly unblemished—simply a gentle healer and a person of courage and honesty. That he apparently had a tyrannical and sadistic side, and that he was even guilty of a degree of fraudulence in his account of his early training and personal history, naturally surprised me when I first learned of it. Then, like many people, I even came to associate his suicide in 1990, at the age of eighty-six, as somehow having been connected with the same conflicts in his nature that had led to his fabricating some false credentials for himself and exaggerating the success of his methods, mistreating some of those in his care, and perhaps even plagiarizing key passages in *The Uses of Enchantment* (a charge that was not substantiated). Yet the death of his wife and the permanent loss of his ability to work resulting from his failing health would surely have been sufficient causes for his choosing to opt out of life when he did.

When I reread many of his writings in recent years and watched him speaking in two BBC documentaries made in the mid-1980s on the Orthogenic School, I found it impossible not to admire aspects of Bettelheim's work, or the insights into human personality it embodied. If he was able to effect cures, or even partial cures, of many in his care, it is a reminder that what we call "autistic symptoms," like most psychological and physiological symptoms, can have many causes (genetic, prenatal, perinatal, postnatal, and in every combination), and while often remaining unaffected by treatment, can sometimes respond to it, or even abate as a result of life experiences. It is a reminder of what may sometimes be achieved if one is able to give a disturbed person devoted attention over many years, under conditions that allow one to respond to what their symptoms are expressing rather than to simply suppress them.

In *Autism: Explaining the Enigma*, Frith recounts how in 1989, at the end of the Ceaușescu reign in Romania, approximately 165 infant orphans, between the ages of approximately six and eighteen months old, were rescued from horrific conditions of deprivation and neglect in Romanian institutions and were adopted into English families, where their progress was carefully tracked and studied. When they arrived in England the children were "malnourished and unresponsive." After reaching the age of four, there were still eleven of the children who "exhibited features that were strongly reminiscent of autism: . . . difficulties in forming normal social relationships . . . impaired language." They were "preoccupied with smelling and touching things . . . and had intense circumscribed interests, for instance in watches, vacuum cleaners, or plumbing." But even these eleven had made a partial or complete recovery from this state by the age of six, confirming, in Frith's words, "that they did not in fact have autism. Instead they suffered from a developmental delay in aspects of social and nonsocial development that can mimic autism." Later she explains this as a kind of "quasi-autism": "A combination of intellectual impairment and prolonged social and sensory deprivation may lead to reversible arrest in the development of particular brain systems." But "in true autism the brain systems themselves are faulty and do not develop properly even in the presence of ample stimulation. In contrast, the brain systems in cases of 'quasi-autism' prove capable of recovery as soon as adequate stimulation is provided."

In his writings Bettelheim suggests that there is what might be called a "ripple effect" in a family where there is a disabled child. While not holding the mother exclusively to blame for the child's anxious withdrawal from the world, as some of his detractors claim he did, he does emphasize that the relationship between parent and child is reciprocal, quoting Anna Freud: "A mother may be experienced as rejecting by the infant for a multitude of different reasons, connected with either her conscious or unconscious attitudes, her bodily or mental defects, her physical presence or absence, her unavoidable libidinal preoccupations, her aggressions, her anxieties, etc. . . . [She] can influence, distort and determine development [in the child], but she cannot produce either neurosis or psychosis." To which Bettelheim adds, "Thus the child's initial autistic reaction can be brought about by a variety of conditions, but whether this temporary reaction becomes a chronic disease depends on the environment's response."

Even though the person most involved in originally studying Mary, Herta Wertheim, who had herself been a student of Anna Freud, was convinced that autism was a brain disorder, an underlying suspicion that a damaged child was a reflection of damaged parents surely scarred my parents, and may even have psychologically distanced them from Mary. In some cases, my parents' included, an aspect of the ripple effect Bettelheim alluded to may have stemmed from his own theories: the needless guilt felt by parents of the genetically impaired.

In the weeks and months following my first solo visit to Briarcliff I alternated between moments of understanding and confusion. I grasped that so much more has been learned about the brain since my childhood. It is better understood now that like linguistic ability, or the ability to focus attention, or memory, or a thousand other faculties, social awareness and the ability to identify with others are not simply acquired in early life but are cultivated in brain areas specifically prepared for them. Our brains are primed to make us identify with others. (For example, I read about so-called mirror neurons, which are said to be activated in "normal" brains when we are observing or hearing of others in human activities. These mirror neurons spark sympathetic physical and emotional responses in us and help us to "identify.")

And I finally grasped that people like Mary tend to be born with deficiencies in these brain areas, and that these deficiencies are usually genetic in origin, even if the exact genetic pathways still remain too multiple and complex to be completely understood. This was reaffirmed by a conversation I had more recently with Dr.

Abha Gupta, an associate research scientist in the Department of Pediatrics and Child Study Center at the Yale University School of Medicine. I asked her what we know at this point about the genetic underpinnings of autism. She told me that "ninety percent of the clinical variation (the way the disorder presents in people) is estimated to be due to genetic variation, which gives autism spectrum disorders the strongest evidence for a genetic basis among all complex neuropsychiatric disorders, including depression, bipolar disorder, and schizophrenia. Twin studies suggest that the etiology of autism spectrum disorders is heavily skewed toward genetics, although environmental factors may also very well be involved. At the same time," she explained, "heritability" is a far more complex matter than most people realize. Research into the precise genetic origins of the various aspects of autism suggests a variety of routes to the condition. "Currently no one gene (or even a few genes) definitively explains a substantial proportion of cases," she continued. "About ten to twenty percent of cases are associated with specific gene mutations, genetic syndromes, and chromosomal abnormalities. However, individually these genetic conditions contribute to only one or two percent of cases. Examples include Fragile X (which causes intellectual disability), tuberous sclerosis (which causes brain abnormalities among other defects), mutations in the synaptic gene *SHANK3*, and copy number variation at the chromosomal locus 16p11. There are a handful of candidate genes with varying levels of evidence for association with autism. If all this sounds imprecise, it is because dissecting the genetic etiology of a disorder as clinically and genetically heterogeneous as autism is very challenging. However, we are making progress. For example, a number of those candidates are converging on the neural synapse, which is no big surprise since the synapse is the fundamental functional unit of the central nervous system. That gives us insight into the pathophysiology of the disorder and suggests the possibility of someday developing more targeted treatments. The story with Fragile X, Rett syndrome, and tuberous sclerosis, which are now better understood and for which new treatments are being developed, gives us inspiration."

Both Kanner and Asperger noted parallels between some of the personality traits of their "autistic" subjects and those of their parents. According to Frith, "as convincing evidence for the genetic causes of autism has now emerged," it is becoming clear that "their clinical intuitions" about this "were not mistaken. Well-controlled studies have shown that fathers as well as mothers may have some of the same traits as their children, often in very mild form."

Brett S. Abrahams and Daniel H. Geschwind, writing in May 2008 in the journal *Nature Reviews Genetics*, put the familial link this way:

> Autism has a strong genetic basis. Several lines of evidence support genetic factors as a predominant cause of the ASDs [autism spectrum disorders]. First is the growing body of literature demonstrating that mutations or structural variation in any of several genes can dramatically increase disease risk. Second, the relative risk of a child being diagnosed with autism is increased at least 25-fold over the population prevalence in families in which a sibling is affected. Third, siblings and parents of an affected child are more likely than controls to show subtle cognitive or behavioural features that are qualitatively similar to those observed in probands [the individuals originally diagnosed as having the disorder]. . . . Fourth, independent twin studies, although small, indicate that concordance

rates for monozygotic twins (70–90%) are several-fold higher than the corresponding values for dizygotic twins (0–10%).

I will probably always have to make a conscious effort to connect the Mary who is a part of my life with the scientific information about "mental retardation" and "autism" I have learned. Despite what are called her "autistic features," Mary is far from oblivious to the world around her, and often seems extraordinarily present and engaged. For the most part, she looks at people when they speak to her. She often smiles. At the same time, her impatience and nervousness and frustration, even her unexplained laughs and bursts of muttered commentary, are constant reminders of forces and reactions within her that remain mysterious.

The textbooks about autism are written by the non-autistic. Intelligence tests are designed by the neurological "winners," the verbal. What about those things that cannot be understood from outside and cannot be measured? Sometimes whole inner worlds come to light in those who can barely speak. A case in point is the music composed unexpectedly in later life by the Japanese author Kenzaburo Oe's nearly nonverbal autistic son. Fortunately there are the writings by Temple Grandin and Gunilla Gerland and a precious few others on the "autistic spectrum" who can speak first-hand about themselves. But since limited communication skills and difficulties with social interaction are at the heart of the condition, it is rare to have a chance to hear from autistic people about their own experience of being alive.

I suppose that even if I will never be able to "understand" her in normal terms, I still balk at defining Mary in terms of what is broken about her, and I don't want to, any more than I want to define myself as only a person with phobias, or as only a short person. She is who she is.

When I return home from my first trip back to Briarcliff by myself, I can't help starting to try to reconstruct the path our two lives have taken, looking at our stories through the lens of our twinship. If I remain resistant to categorizing Mary, I tell myself, it is probably because diagnoses are by definition rough, flawed generalizations. The "abnormal" are as inconsistent in their ways as the "normal." When you look closely at anyone, they transcend type. Everyone is on a spectrum. Everyone breaks the rules.

3

TOGETHER

Apparently many more people start out in their mother's womb with a twin who never becomes a newborn than is commonly realized. Although experts on development differ about whether or not "twin loss" that occurs in utero leaves a psychological imprint in its wake, there is no disagreement about the fact that roughly 12 percent of pregnancies begin as twin pregnancies and only 2 percent of those result in twin births. Identical twins occur when one zygote (fertilized egg) splits into two embryos (usually within the first thirteen days after conception). So-called fraternal twins, created from two eggs fertilized by two sperm, are three times more common than identical ones but, unlike them, are more common in some cultures than in others. For example, the Yoruba tribe in Nigeria give birth to twins in one out of eleven pregnancies. Such "dizygotic" twins are no more genetically alike than any two siblings. That is, they each share 50 percent of each parent's DNA, as all siblings do. They are also in the "vast majority of cases" separated by being in two amniotic sacs during gestation, with a thin membrane between them.

Nevertheless, according to Alessandra Piontelli, who has summarized prenatal twin development in her book *Twins: From Fetus to Child*, even in what she describes as a life "more akin to oblivion . . . than to alertness," the developing twins begin to affect each other through their motions "as early as nine weeks." At fourteen weeks from conception, twins are already rehearsing such motions as stroking their faces and taking small steps, often kicking their co-twin and causing their instinctive "rooting response. Amazingly, but not surprisingly, the behavior patterns discerned in each twin during intrauterine life through ultrasounds appear to correlate to those after birth. 'Torpid' twins remain so, 'jittery' ones remain jittery," as do "easily 'excited' ones."

Our amnesia about early childhood makes it almost seem as if it takes years for the prenatal "oblivion" to wear off. We do not recall the shock of birth, and there is a kind of childhood fog that surrounds every memory from early life, no matter how vivid our experiences actually were, with a dreamlike haze. Surely all the intense learning and bonding and sensing and seeking of one's first days was all the more stingingly vital for being brand-new. We certainly bear the scars and reflect the impact of the time forever.

Summer 1948, August 27: 12:57 a.m., Mary is born; 1:02 a.m., I am born. We are six weeks premature. Our mother had lost two babies in previous pregnancies, one a few years before, and the other a few years after my brother's birth. She is ecstatic. Our father is home with a cold. He and our five-year-old brother receive the news of the twin births over the phone—"Twins! A boy and a girl!" Twins were usually a surprise in those days, and they are astonished. We are tiny by ancestry, by being twins, and by being

born so early. We weigh four pounds each. We are put in incubators and stay there for six weeks. After all these many days in the
hospital we are home. Our father, who had once thought that the
world was too difficult a place to bring more people into it, but who
after eighteen years of marriage had finally changed his mind, is
now lifting us over his head in joy and amazement. Our brother,
dressed in a white short-sleeved shirt and corduroy dungarees, is
posing for pictures holding the two of us, one in each arm.

In third or fourth grade, asked to write our "autobiographies," I
recalled an early memory: standing in front of an amorphous red
blob I had painted and saying that it was a witch. In my recollec-
tion, friends of my parents, holding drinks in their hands, were
asking me to explain who the witch was.

Later in this "autobiography" I referred to a memory that actually had to have come from an earlier time. My sister and I were in
adjoining cribs, and we were rocking backwards and forwards in
unison. We were knocking our heads gently but repeatedly on the
headboards. I wrote about this "nightly ritual" at some length, in-
nocent of sex, but still cognizant that the experience was private,
collaborative, and even intense. That I called it a "ritual" shows that
I instinctively knew the activity to be stabilizing, soothing, and
necessary. This was a nightly routine in the period before my sister
and I slept in separate rooms. If I close my eyes to my current world
and responsibilities, I can imagine that I am back there, on all
fours, peering through the white slats of my crib at Mary's rocking
form, blurry in the dark, but still visible by the Manhattan streetlights coming through the venetian blinds. I can even hear the
squeaking of the beds, hear the sound of the headboards being
struck, and feel the mattress under my knees.

But it is amazing how little else I can locate in my memory from my first three years, and strange that I would find only this one nightly activity and a lone red inkblot there when I search.

In fact, we initially shared the same crib, and the ritual may well have begun there. We napped and slept together. We also shared a double stroller when we were taken out for walks in the sunlight of Central Park. We were fed at the same time. My brother still remembers feeding us simultaneously.

In photos from our infancy, Mary is taller and plumper than I am, and tends to look calmer than I do. I appear irked and restless when being held—eager to wriggle free—whereas she seems docile and dreamy. The distinction that seems obvious looking at the photos today is that I am focusing outward, looking around me, whereas she could be described as lost in thought. Our brother, five years older, is already a seasoned extrovert, with a wide variety of grins, smirks, and waves, and some expressions that could only be characterized as ironic. Home movies taken when we are in our first year show Mary crawling more slowly than I do, and in one, when I roll over my head in an infant somersault, she attempts a similar move, but only partially completes it.

I don't remember Mary starting to show any distress at this age. While I remember her screaming and running through the halls of the apartment as a five- or six-year-old, I have no sense of her unhappiness, if she did display it, as an infant or toddler. Sharing a room with her remains only the vaguest memory, more a feeling of textures and sensations—like the proximity of her small warm form in frilly outfits—than a memory per se. I remember the comforting feeling of having her nearby, as if her presence was central, a point of rest. But I would only strain the limits of language trying to describe the sensation. Even now I am more relaxed in her company than at any other time.

I know now that sometime during her first year my parents started to worry about Mary. Apparently she did not smile until she was six months old and did not engage in play with adults when I did. She seemed entranced by objects, but not particularly responsive to or curious about people. Even more than in the case of the average infant, her concentration would fix on the immediate detail. At six months she would put small objects to her nose to smell. At twelve to fifteen months, she spent long periods staring at individual toys, or at her hand. Her fascination with hands has in fact been lifelong. As a child, she particularly liked staring at our father's large hands and was fascinated by the way they looked when he was playing the piano.

Even in our first year when we were taken for walks to Central Park in our double stroller, or placed in adjoining playpens, our parents apparently noticed additional discrepancies in our progress through the expected developmental stages. But their worries still centered more on what they assumed was their inability to engage Mary or make her happy than on whether she was innately impaired in some way. They were well aware that no two infants develop the same way or at the same rate.

Sometime in our second year her comparative unresponsiveness made them worry that she had a hearing impairment. That her hearing was in fact acute was later borne out by her ability to pick out melodies at the piano and her love of singing along with recordings of musicals (particularly *Oklahoma!*) and operas (*Lucia di Lammermoor*), as well as her sensitivity to noises, including her own shouts. At an early age Mary's coordination was also tested. I remember her walking up and down the few steps of a wooden platform the size of a conductor's podium for hours at a time, which was a physical therapy that had been recommended for her. By the age of two and a half her limited use of words caused her pediatrician concern, and he recommended that she be studied by a psychologist who was an expert in speech development. I remember watching a gentle young woman sitting with Mary at a small wooden table, asking her to do drawings and color in shapes with crayons. I remember Mary's hair being braided by Bessie, my parents' cook and housekeeper; the mysterious world of her costume jewelry, like the plastic pearls that popped into place to form bracelets and necklaces; her little dresses and black-buckled party shoes.

I also remember the inwardness and inner-directed quality of her speech, her muttered dialogue with herself; her constant preoccupation with her right arm, which she would repeatedly kiss and then pause to look at, smiling to herself, before resuming to kiss it; her sometimes raw, chewed-on fingers; the start-and-stop quality her walking sometimes had, as if she were always reconsidering where she was going. I remember her tranquillity, but also how it would shift unexpectedly. Sometimes the cause of her frustration would be apparent, like a plastic pearl falling from her grasp under the bed. And when the situation was righted, she would be contented again. But at other times a tension would seem to mount inside her that had more the character of a meteorological event, and she would start to speak in a tense, strident voice, sometimes repeating phrases ("Mary Shawn is not going to the park"), which could have been wishes that called for reassurances, or failed attempts to express some mysterious pain. She had a sideways, dark look sometimes, as if perceiving a threat or something ominous. If she were resisting doing something, she could start to kick and scream, and sometimes ran through the hallway holding her ears and yelling. I remember seeing my mother trying to hold her when she was kicking and crying out. I remember seeing her in a beautiful dress at one of our birthday parties, and the contrast between the pretty pink dress she was wearing and the green berets in her hair and her desperate mood and tears of exasperation.

The sound of Mary's screaming has stayed with me. When I first had children of my own, their cries upset me more than they should have, and I needed to be reminded that babies cry simply because that is their only way of expressing distress.

From the moment my parents realized for certain that there was something the matter with Mary, they put me in my own room down the hall from her, with my brother's room between us, and began to shield me from her. It became less common for them to refer to us as twins. They began to protect me from her and encourage me to think of myself as simply an individual.

Like most children, I knew very little—and thought very little—about what my parents were going through when they were bringing me up. (I knew nothing about the additional complexities in my father's life until I was close to thirty.) Nevertheless, I became aware of issues surrounding the raising of children earlier than some people do. From an early age I intuited that there were tensions surrounding Mary and instinctively took it upon myself to continue to be the easier child and avoid worrying my parents.

Mary loved repetition, even more than most children do. She played the same recordings again and again on a child's square-shaped phonograph the size of a small suitcase, which had little holes on the side from which the music issued. She communed with Maria Callas and sang along with Joan Sutherland performing the mad scene from Donizetti's *Lucia di Lammermoor*. She particularly liked opera scenes that were, in fact, mad scenes. Her singing is not easy to describe. It was more like a sympathetic vocal accompaniment to what she was hearing—partly sung, partly moaned, partly murmured, almost like Schoenberg's *Sprechstimme* (speech-song) in *Pierrot Lunaire*. We went to the movie version of *Oklahoma!* five times. More than fifty years later she will still launch into her version of the opening number if someone else starts to sing it.

Her crying would often escalate at night, and since I was in my own room after the age of three, and in between my room and Mary's was my brother's room, this often kept my brother awake. Mary's bursts of unhappiness were unfathomable and not easy to assuage. The search for the origins of her misery, or for a way to comfort or distract her, could last for hours.

Even after we each had our own room, we still played alongside each other, forming the base of the triangle of which our older brother was the peak. Mary and I would sit at a small table doing drawings together, and I remember how she would fill page after page with circular motions of a crayon, or sometimes single lines. Once she drew colorful lines across the spines of our father's new twenty-volume *Oxford English Dictionary*.

Our social lives began to diverge when I started attending Dalton nursery school and she went uptown to a nursery school at Riverside Church. She did play with other children, but only with those who were younger than she was.

I remember nothing of my parents' concerns about Mary, only

that they told me that she was "slow." At a certain point I began hearing the term "mentally retarded" used about her. There were moments when the word "autism" was used too. Because I now have the documents my mother saved about her, I see that she was first officially diagnosed in June 1955 when she was six by Dr. William S. Langford, a renowned child psychiatrist and pediatrician, an expert in children's "emotional problems," who worked at Presbyterian Medical Center. In a letter written later he noted that at that time Mary could feed herself, dress herself "using buttons," work out simple jigsaw puzzles, and that she had been toilet trained the previous year, "after some struggle." But while she "could count three or four objects," she could not put many words together in combination when she spoke, and in fact rarely spoke as if trying to communicate. When asked a question, she tended to repeat it. Recently she had learned to answer "Does Mary want a cookie" with "Mary wants a cookie?" His interpretation was that she was showing "secondary autistic features associated with being brain damaged."

With teachers and friends at school I gradually became self-conscious when I was asked if I had brothers and sisters. It seemed impossible to simultaneously convey both the information that I had a twin sister—which always provoked excitement—along with the news that she was "mentally retarded," which caused awkward looks of shock and sympathy. When I got both bits of information across with sufficient speed I could avoid causing an embarrassing collision of emotional responses in my questioner. But meanwhile my own discomfort would be acute. A sense of anxiety came to enshroud this basic fact of my existence, as must happen to children who are adopted, or whose parents are dead or imprisoned. Sometimes I lied by omission, cheerfully saying only that I had an older brother. Yet the lie weighed on me; it was a betrayal. I felt deeply uncomfortable when people told me how sorry they were that my twin was "retarded." What was impossible to explain to anyone was that while Mary's condition was a tragedy in our parents' lives, for me it did not constitute a "loss." Mary, exactly as she was, was an integral part of my world. I had a complete sister, whose strangeness in terms of certain norms had only gradually become known to me.

The stereotypical description of the autistic child does not quite jibe with my recollections of Mary at the age of seven. If she did not communicate verbally at her age level, she did connect to others through the piercingly direct look she could give with her brown eyes; her memory of everyone's names; her unexpected smiles and laughter; her looks of amusement; her responsiveness to pictures and movies and music; her way of laying claim to us by gripping our arms and clasping our hands. Even now, in middle age, while she accepts a hug only rather stiffly and grudgingly, she will still grab my chin in her characteristic way and plant a kiss on my cheek. To her naïve brothers she almost gave the sense that she was holding herself back, that deep down she was verbal and full of understanding, but that she just couldn't present that side of herself to the world. (Likewise, the mother of "Richard M." in Kanner's groundbreaking 1943 article said of her son, "He gave the impression of silent wisdom to me.") It is no wonder that in the 1950s, when such children were still often viewed as emotionally disturbed rather than neurologically impaired, there was a sense of confusion in the household about whether Mary might someday be cured of whatever spell had been cast over her.

As children we rode tricycles together, we danced when our father played the piano. On Christmas (which we celebrated for its décor, food, and sense of magic, despite our Jewish ancestry), Mary and I and our brother sat on the living room floor under the tree opening our presents. Although I cannot remember a single one of our joint birthday parties in any detail, I still remember the fun of the three of us sitting under the Christmas tree with its sparkling lights and tearing through the colorful wrappings, and carefully taking each item out of the stockings we had hung the night before that our father had filled with marbles, bubble gum, Tootsie Rolls, playing cards, tiny figurines, and an orange at the bottom. Mary never forgot the holidays we celebrated in the apartment, and in later years and decades our mother never neglected to send her all the things she would remember having received at home as each holiday came along in the year's calendar.

Bessie took us regularly to the park. I remember Mary running happily on the grass. I remember the time I forgot to change into my shoes and looked down to find myself in my blue bedroom slippers in the middle of a field, and how I cried from humiliation and needed to be carried home. I remember having at least as many misadventures in the world as Mary did. But I also remember that sometimes Mary would have an outburst and lie down on the sidewalk and scream.

At other times, she seemed completely self-contained and to mirror our father's gift for intense concentration. At the age of five she could sit still for hours at a time, coupling and uncoupling beads in a necklace, methodically drawing her rough swirls of color with crayons on thick yellow paper, playing with her dolls, or placing tiny pieces of furniture in the toy dollhouse in her room. My mother and Bessie always made sure that her hair was carefully brushed or crisply braided and that she was neatly dressed. Sometimes she was left that way entirely alone in her room. She seemed, at such peaceful moments, able to entirely shut out the world, as our father could when he was editing. Seated on the floor, occupied and calm, she looked beautiful and contemplative. With her translucent skin, broad forehead, and light brown, almond-shaped eyes, dressed so carefully, she could have been a princess in a fairy tale.

Our mother buzzed with cheerful activity much of the time, and was never for a moment visibly depressed, yet seemed to struggle to keep her mind focused when she had a moment to read or think. I know now how brilliant and utterly original she was—I can easily picture her as the attractive, adventurous, and independent young career woman our father had fallen in love with and looked up to back in 1925, when they first met—but then it almost seemed as if she didn't want to be valued for her own talents or intelligence, but only as a wife and mother. A former journalist, she had retained her keen mind for politics, her ability to remember information and statistics, and her gift for argument, but one also had the sense—even I as a child had the sense—of something distracting her from using these gifts. Naturally she was tired. Under any circumstances, raising a family is hard. But one sensed that there was more to her mental restiveness than simply fatigue and normal family pressures.

When we were all under one roof, our five personalities vibrated each in its own way, causing a kind of collective hum. Often we five were in five separate rooms. My childhood friend Hank remembers playing with me one day and being astonished when he happened to open Mary's door, finding her there, seated on the floor, playing quietly.

Only now as I write this do I notice what Mary and I didn't do together. Although I have vivid memories of Halloween—down to the pinching tightness of the leotard onto which my mother had sewn the beautiful alligator costume she constructed for me when I was six—I don't remember Halloween with Mary. She was often off by herself, even off-limits. When my friends would come over to play with me, most of them, like Hank, tended to regard Mary with a kind of awe and a tender reverence. This was particularly the case with my friend David, who was my classmate at school, as was his own twin sister. Not surprisingly, Mary was of interest to David, and he never failed to ask after her. I remember his standing in the hallway peering thoughtfully into her room, where she was playing with blocks on the floor. David, who as an adult is a successful theater producer, seemed to me as a child to possess all the attributes of an ideal person. He was handsome, tall, articulate, and popular. To me, he exuded a kind of heroic normality. Next to his authoritative sturdiness, I felt emboldened and protected.

Even as a child you can lay claim to a subject with the zealousness of a professional. By such standards my early childhood interests were those of a dilettante. I did once write to Walt Disney requesting a job as a cartoonist and enclosed some of my drawings. In return, I received a humblingly generic oversized postcard, thanking me for my interest in Mickey Mouse, Goofy, and Donald Duck, with Walt Disney's printed signature at the bottom. However, it is amusing to remember that my drawings were appreciated enough by my classmates to create a reputation. During free periods at school I offered "classes," and friends would sit with me around a table, imitating my drawings of people, an early rehearsal for the actual teaching I ended up doing from the age of twenty-five until today.

For a few years, inspired by a science project at school, I collected rocks. I was intrigued by their variety and by the way they revealed their origins in different eras of the earth's history. Later it was maps—a fascination I have retained, and which creates a kind of cognitive dissonance with my rampant travel fears. I adored baseball and made scrapbooks of baseball pictures from newspapers and *Sports Illustrated*. When my father improvised jazz at the piano I would accompany him on the drums—displaying no great talent—while my brother played the violin.

At about the age of seven I began a lengthy story about my friend David. It seemed entirely natural to make him its central protagonist. The story stretched out to become what I called a "novel" of more than a hundred pages and constituted my first concentrated piece of "work." In several chapters I placed David in danger, pitting him against a band of "crooks" whom he eventually vanquished, and I gave him a love interest transparently modeled on Tom Sawyer's flirtation with Becky Thatcher. In the book the first sentence and the last were the same, ending with David's name, as if the mere stating of his name, his centrality to the story, carried some lyrical weight. But even though there was, in a sense, no actual literary impulse behind this writing, I still remember the exhilaration of completing it a full year after beginning it, that same feeling of having given form to something that I later got from writing music, a sense of a lightness in the air, of a task accomplished, of the warm spring air wafting through my window, telling me that the world belonged particularly to me. It was at least another forty years before I recognized in my idealization of David a wish to have, as he did, a twin sister with whom I could have a normal conversation, and with whom I could go to school.

Despite or because of Mary's daily proximity, I had an early tendency to choose mates. At five I proposed marriage to my classmate Lucy and brought her flowers. This naturally did not lead anywhere, except that it initiated a rash of flower giving on the part of my male classmates. At six I went further, inviting a girl over with the express purpose of secretly undressing her. The girl in question had previously disrobed for no apparent reason in art class, thus sparking my desire to request a private experience of my own with her. In the scene that ensued in my own bedroom, we took off our clothes and felt for where we differed from each other. Her silky pouch of softness, in the place where I had my own squishy appendage, was wondrous. We were naked as worms in the semidark, only to be surprised by the sound of footsteps in the hall and the sudden, harsh light of discovery. My mother considered this a man's issue, to be dealt with by my father. A hushed feeling came over the household as we awaited his return from work for any possible punishment, reproach, or word of caution. I remember sitting next to him on the sofa in the living room, looking at his serious face, sensing what seemed like a terrible weariness in him. He summarized his views kindly yet enigmatically: "There was nothing wrong with what you did," he said, "we just don't do it."

In this era long before electronic games and when television was still new and off-limits for most of the day, childhood play tended to be creative and hands-on. If in play with Mary I needed to double as an interpreter, in play with friends I was frequently a court jester, alternating as comedian and straight man in comic skits. Performing for whoever would watch was our way of having fun and breaking free from all constraints. With my friend Jay I explored the joys of the idiotic, the disgusting, the primitive, and the elaborately, if innocently, violent. There was as much pleasure in pretending to be shot in a gunfight in Central Park and dramatically rolling downhill and landing in a limp heap in the soft spring grass as there was in sledding down the same hill in the winter snow. We would do our routines—a favorite was for me to interview Jay as an average "man on the street"—for our mothers, for our friends, or just for ourselves. Without knowing it, we were satirizing adult life. Often we would type up imaginary news stories or ridiculous accounts and make ourselves laugh. More surprisingly, perhaps, I didn't need an audience or even a friend to put on productions. For several years, starting when I was about seven, I imagined that I had my own television show and would retreat into my room to present this to my imaginary audience. I prepared for each episode quite seriously, spending my allowance money on required production materials, even though no one saw the results. The line between pretending to have an audience and actually having one was never crystal clear to me—an issue raised by many a contemporary music concert I participated in, in later years—and neither was the line between the emotions stirred by acting and those stirred by real life. There were moments in our skits, as in the little films and puppet shows I later did with my brother, when an intense sadness would well up in me when I was called upon to look sad or even mock-sad, or when an unbridled fury would overtake me in the act of only mimicking anger. Acting taught me something that involvement in music later confirmed: that there were wells of emotion in people. You simply had to think a certain way and a bucket would drop down into the well inside you and come back filled with feeling.

Our family rented a summer house each year in Bronxville, New York, close enough to the city for my father to be driven every day to work, but bucolic enough for my mother to spend long hours outside in the sun in her sleeveless outfits, tending a small garden of zinnias and sunflowers, and wax and green beans. Our mother came to life in the presence of the greenery of the trees. Perhaps it wasn't the natural world that thrilled her so much as the greenness itself. She had studied painting at the Art Students League in Chicago when she was in her early teens—sent there by her frugal, widowed mother who worked at the post office—and she had retained a lifelong love of painting, an activity she also resumed each summer in painting classes. She was a light-and-color person. She would gasp with pleasure at the colors in flowers, in paintings, in movies, or onstage in sets and costumes. In the city, she waited all year with anticipation for the spring, when the yellow forsythia and white cherry blossoms would bloom briefly in the park, and would sigh and point to them when we drove through the park transverses separating the East and West sides. She took pride in the boxes of hydrangeas she planted overlooking Fifth Avenue. When we arrived in Bronxville in late June she would be dazzled by the trees, and she would exclaim, "The trees . . . the trees . . ." over and over again. A kind of serenity came over her in Bronxville.

Despite being only five miles from Manhattan, Bronxville did bring us closer to nature. The night sky looked far blacker than it ever did in the city and was often filled with glittering constellations and, in August, shooting stars. There were combustible storms foreshadowed by an overcast sky tinged a deep olive green in midday, followed by colossal rips and booms of thunder, electric flashes of lightning, and torrents of unimpeded rain. The way the storms seemed to gather themselves out of their own forces, stirring the enormous trees, swirling currents of wind and clattering rainfall, physicalized a power that was thrillingly beyond human control.

It was in summertime that the distinction between Mary's and my educational paths ceased to matter very much. Even though my brother and I attended "Camp Mohawk" in White Plains, a camp that in many ways each of us hated, there were still many times when the three of us played together. Sundays, when our father did not go to the city, were particularly memorable. He would sometimes stay in his pajamas and bathrobe most of the day, and even on a warm day work in a lawn chair outside. Mary and I would ride tricycles while our brother rode his big-boy's bike, or the three of us would splash in a small inflatable pool. Sometimes we set up croquet wickets and the entire family, our father included, would play. The distinctive clicks of the heavy striped croquet balls would resonate in the afternoon air. The family occasionally drove to get ice cream or play miniature golf, and these were the times we actually witnessed our father at the wheel of a car.

As I made my way from one grade to the next, Mary was tried out at a series of schools. After age five, she did not progress to first grade but remained in kindergarten, as each year she grew older and bigger than her classmates. She also resisted many aspects of the daily school routine. It seemed clear to her teachers that, just as she could not hold complicated conversations, she could not follow complicated directions, and that if she were going to make progress in basic arithmetic or learning to read, she would need a kind of special, individualized instruction they couldn't offer. I sensed the tension surrounding Mary and school, the perpetual question of what to do. I instinctively sensed that she was socially isolated, even if on occasion a child—always a younger child— came home to play with her. I also recall the physical force with which she would balk at doing something she did not want to; my mother and Bessie both holding her while trying to put on her coat; the sounds of scuffling and her protests. Even with every attempt being made to shield me from it, I must have sensed that it was in fact a desperate situation.

What a difficulty for my parents, in an era when there were few people to whom they could turn for advice about mental illness and brain injury, and little or no grasp of what the prognosis might be for such a child. What a leaden weight it must have been on them to contemplate Mary's future with all the questions her nature raised: Would she deteriorate or improve over time? If she could never sustain herself, who would take care of her? What would happen to her after they—my parents—died? And then the burden of wondering about the cause of her condition.

Dr. Wood, their pediatrician, warned them that disabled children place enormous strains on a marriage. Even without realizing it, he said, each parent blames the other.

I know now that at that time they sought the advice of psychiatrists and psychologists recommended by Dr. Langford. One of these was Herta Wertheim. Wertheim had been born in Czechoslovakia in 1902 and had traveled to Vienna to pursue her interest in Freud and childhood education; she had been a student of Anna Freud's, was briefly analyzed by one of her students, and later became the director of Dr. Freud's nursery school in Vienna. She had fled Nazi persecution in 1938, the same year Sigmund Freud and his family had fled Vienna for London. (The Freuds made it a point to oversee the escape of those who worked for them before they left Vienna themselves.) Dr. Wertheim visited Mary regularly over a period of two years when Mary was four to five years old. She was accustomed to severely disturbed preschool children from her work as director of the Putnam Center in Roxbury, Massachusetts, and the Child Development Center in New York (now part of the Jewish Board of Family and Children's Services), and she described Mary to Langford and others as "a very troubled little girl." Despite her psychiatric orientation, she was opposed to the concept that autism was the responsibility or fault of the parents. She believed that it was essentially an organic condition. Yet at the same time she hoped for Mary's at least partial recovery.

But in terms of what could be done for Mary at that time and in that environment to actually make her happy in her home or school life, the situation must often have appeared to be increasingly discouraging and exhausting. She did not have friends. Her needs were often incomprehensible, and her outbursts often dominated my parents' attention and drained their energies. Mary was a big child and could be fierce when she was unhappy. Although never aggressive toward people, she could still be destructive and self-destructive. At the age of six or seven, she sometimes smeared the walls with her feces. She bit her arm and tore the skin around her fingernails. My parents, who could only rarely manage to comfort Mary or feel that they understood her, increasingly placed her in the care of Bessie, who was physically stronger than they were and had an intuitive understanding of her. Since she was not Mary's parent, Bessie was probably less overwhelmed by the responsibility entrusted to her, and certainly less disturbed by the issues Mary's condition potentially raised. Having no children of her own, she wholeheartedly and unequivocally loved the three of us. My friend Jay remembers Mary banging angrily on the keys of the piano, and Bessie gently yet firmly hustling her away to her own room.

Entirely unbeknownst to me at the time, my mother was making a heroic effort to cope with this situation and figure out what to do about it. It was horribly difficult. Once she blurted out to a friend, "I wish someone would just tell me what is wrong!"

It was Dr. Wertheim who suggested that my parents contact an expert in child development in Massachusetts named Irene Anderson. Miss Anderson, who had master's degrees in psychology and social work, and experience in analytic training with children, was founding a summer camp for "mentally disturbed" youngsters of elementary school age. My parents made contact with her sometime in late 1956 or early 1957.

Not much is understood about the difference between the attachment fraternal twins tend to have to each other and that of siblings generally, or whether one can generalize at all about the relationship. By contrast, clichés about identical twins are widespread: one has heard startling stories of orphaned twins sent to different continents at the age of one month who, without even knowing of each other's existence, grow up to marry similar women, pursue parallel careers, and have matching hobbies. A celebrated example is the case of the reunited "Jim twins" studied at the University of Minnesota who, without knowing each other since infancy, had, among many other things, married women with the same name, frequently vacationed at the same vacation spot, worked part-time as sheriffs, enjoyed woodworking, and bit their fingernails in exactly the same way. The lore of fraternal twins—who share DNA in the same proportion as regular siblings—is less spectacular but still suggests a bond that far outweighs mere genetics. Some studies of opposite-sex fraternal twins tend to suggest a tendency for the females to dominate, and for the males to exhibit traits once considered more feminine. This could be the result of hormonal exchanges in utero, or from mutual influence in early life. But simply by sharing the same early routines at the same time, such as feeding and bedtime and play, and going through the same early stages in tandem, twins of any kind develop patterns of cooperation, collaboration, and competition earlier than, and perhaps different than, those of other children.

By definition, I learned only gradually that living with Mary posed a "challenge." My character was formed by early interactions in which accommodation to her inwardness and anguish were automatic. I do know that when I began to speak, I was the one who often told the adults what it was that Mary was asking for, and it was a role I found myself taking on when I first went to school and encountered little playmates who were hard to understand. An early childhood friend was a Japanese girl, Yukiko, who brought me presents of colorful Japanese children's books with glossy, painted pages made of sturdy cardboard. I remember teachers asking me if I could explain to them what Yukiko was trying to say, and in fact being able to. I wonder now if, like an infant in a bilingual home, I hadn't instinctively learned two languages by the time I was verbal, one unspoken one for communicating with Mary, and the other for communicating with everyone else.

At home I surely learned I was male by comparing myself to Mary. I remember the contrast between her belongings and the things in my room—the lead soldiers, forts, toy guns, pink rubber balls, baseball mitts, rocks, coonskin hats—and then the later vanishing of this contrast, as if all the colors in the house had been replaced by shades of grey. I must have sought to confirm this maleness with the girl I invited over. But while I was the one who had inherited our father's large ears—she shared my mother's and brother's tidy, seashell ears, as well as something of the texture of our mother's hair—otherwise I looked more like my mother, while Mary's facial features linked her to our father's side of the family.

Mary retains to this day a resemblance to my father and brother. When she was still present in the house, these connections made her a mirror in which my parents and brother saw aspects of themselves. She was a constant reminder of the handiwork of nature.

When she lived at home, Mary acted as a kind of glue connecting my parents and my brother and me. She kept alive a current of emotional, animal communication between us. With her we were creaturely, bound by blood, by chemistry. Without her, we became four individuals, bound, too much of the time, by words.

All childhoods are normal to the child. I don't remember ever consciously wishing for Mary to be other than as she was. In our different ways both my brother and I were as used to Mary's companionship as we were to each other's. Tormented as our parents were about what to do about Mary, they made every effort not to place this burden on us. Even if we intuited the strain of it, we knew nothing about the decisions they had to confront. Mary was simply our sister, her "deficits" inevitable, and her various moods just a part of daily life, no more under anyone's control than the weather.

4

SUMMER

When I close my eyes and try to walk through the blank space in my mind, trying to remember the summer Mary and I turned nine, I can dimly make out my mother telling us—my brother and myself—that Mary would be going to a summer camp for retarded children. After that, I remember neither the trip in which we all presumably accompanied her there—to "Sandpiper"—nor the moment at the end of the summer when our parents told us that the camp had become a year-round school, and that Mary would be staying there from now on. Of Mary's voyage to a new life I remember precisely nothing. There was certainly no official send-off. Presumably the little my parents said about it was handled in an offhand way, so as not to upset us, and never discussed after that. But I don't remember any of it.

I know only that in the wake of the change, I experienced all the ensuing pains of these growing years as compounding the injury of this one. The dreads and nightmares I had at this age all seemed to revolve around the themes of loss, separation, and travel. Now that the word "camp" had taken on a euphemistic meaning, I daydreamed obsessively of being dragged away from my parents as they were put on trains to concentration camps, which I must have learned about from my brother. I did not understand the concept of loneliness, nor had I been prepared for it. Sometimes I cried myself to sleep, singing a kind of lullaby to myself.

My relationship to my brother also deeply changed. I began to cling to him with admiration and awe, although often expressing this, as younger siblings will, by being annoying. Around this time I saw the movie *The Little Fugitive*, about a boy who mistakenly thinks he has killed his older brother, a plot that so overwhelmed my emotions that when the brothers were reunited at the end I was nearly capsized by my own tears.

My brother, as if by instinct, did his best to include me in his life. He featured me in the home movies he began to make. We also began doing our "puppet shows" together. These were ambitious little productions performed for our parents and guests, with scripts written by my brother, in which we each played all the roles and constructed the sets and characters that appeared inside a little puppet stage. He taught me how to play chess, and this added to our arsenal of game options, which also included canasta, checkers, Monopoly, and, best of all, Clue. We watched late-night movies together on weekends. He wanted me to know all his friends. We went on excursions together. I have a little "viewfinder" that documents from the summer of 1957 my brother and my expedition to the top of the Empire State Building. There we peered through the periscopes at the magical revelation of beautiful New York City below—majestic, peaceful, clean, and dotted with toylike cars in motion—and we made recordings of our voices (mine was probably a rendition of "Hound Dog") and posed for the strip of photos that were put in the viewfinder.

But Mary's departure from our daily life was like an unmourned death. Her absence, the fact that she was elsewhere and would remain so, was not incorporated into our reality, and we all rarely referred to it. After she left, the fact that I was her twin became close to unmentionable. Her picture sat next to mine and my brother's in a framed triptych in the living room; we still referred to "Mary's room," even after it had accumulated our mother's exercise bike, innumerable boxes of old shoes, and shopping bags filled with saved newspapers and magazines. In most ways it felt almost as if Mary had never been a part of our lives, as if the lie I had sometimes spoken when I said I was one of two children, instead of three, had turned out to be true. At our parents' parties, the subject of Mary, for the most part, joined the list of painful unmentionables. On holidays our mother would phone Chatham, Massachusetts, and put me on the phone for ritualized exchanges in which I tried to ask Mary questions she could answer. "Have you been swimming?" "Mary Shawn has been swimming." But our communications had never been primarily verbal, and these types of exchanges were stilted and unfamiliar.

Short letters and cards arrived with painstakingly scripted sentences from Mary and sometimes crayon drawings made, it appeared, from a template provided by a teacher. The letters were written in pen, in a regular handwriting that, while dutiful, was at least Mary's own:

Dear Mommy and daddy—

How are you I went swimming yesterday. I am learning how
to swim we went to holiday lake we had a picnic supper
write soon

Love
mary

And the contents were true, even if coaxed and corrected.
(Mary always referred to herself in the third person. She would not
have written or said, "I went swimming.") All in all she showed
impressive progress. In her first year at the school she learned
enough to become ready for first-grade work, and in the ensuing
years reached a fourth- to fifth-grade level in arithmetic, spelling,
writing, and the mechanics of reading. It was never easy to tell if
Mary comprehended what she read, since she would only repeat
the words back and never attempted to find her own words to sum-
marize the contents. History and geography did not mean anything to her.

It must have taken heroic patience to teach her. Mary had a low
tolerance for being told she had made a mistake. In a letter I now
have in front of me, Miss Anderson wrote, "She reacts to correction verbally insisting that 'Mary is right,' or by throwing a temper
tantrum, kicking her feet, screaming, etc." Perhaps, with no way to
conceptualize the idea of "right" and "wrong" answers, she perceived correction as in its way a violation of the order of things. If
she had answered a question to the best of her ability, perhaps she
felt that she had performed the task expected of her.

Mary sometimes seemed to live within a grid of holidays, often anticipating the entire year's calendar out loud in terms of the upcoming celebrations and the foods associated with them. "October, Mary wants a pumpkin. Easter is coming—Easter egg. November—Turkey." Mary's intense need for predictability was gratified by the school routine but was always under threat. She was intensely vigilant about her environment. While she pursued most recreational activities alone—bicycling, swimming, playing the piano, knitting, crafts—she still wanted people and things to stay in their proper places, and always knew what all the other children were doing, whether or not they had received phone calls, and where they were going on a trip or a visit home. "When a child she has known for a long time is away for a day or even an hour," Miss Anderson wrote,

> she will ask where she is and when she will return. She had no use for a boy her age who graduated two years ago. However as soon as he left, she wanted to know exactly where he was. Frequently in her disturbed states, she will call out the names of many of the children who have left insisting that they come back. . . . At times she seems to be completely out of control, red in the face, shouting or screaming which increases to a kind of frenzy, jumping or throwing her body about.

Fortunately, Miss Anderson seemed to know how to reach her when she was distressed.

In Mary's absence, my parents would always give my brother and me—and each other—presents in her name, which they signed, in block capital letters, "M A R Y." Our father wrote our mother short notes in Mary's behalf ("I Love you, dear Mommy—from Mary"). Many years later my mother said to me that he had given Mary a "voice."

But even though she was very much alive, in the family Mary became a poignant symbol of loss, and was referred to, if at all, wistfully, nostalgically—not as our living sister. If comments about her current life were rare, those about her own subjective experience of the world were virtually nonexistent.

Between the ages of eight and ten I had additional experiences that reinforced my understanding of the unpredictability and sadness of life. My homeroom teacher, a lovely young woman, died unexpectedly over Thanksgiving vacation, and my mother's account of her manner of death ("She suffered from dizzy spells; she opened a window at her doctor's office and fell out") struck me as phony from the moment I heard it. Even then I knew what suicide was, and suspected it. In the same year, an elderly doctor collapsed at my feet on the street, apparently from a heart attack. Within months of experiencing this shock, I was playing in the alleyway to our apartment building with a girl in our building when a man exposed himself to her and began following her as if intending to rape her. When I pushed him and told her to run, I was left alone with him, long enough for me to see that he appeared to be a harmless retarded man, but also long enough for me to feel terribly scared.

Then my pet hamster died.

I became afraid of the dark and afraid of my own imagination, which now generated thoughts of death, haunting apparitions of my dead teacher, and unbidden images of men falling suddenly on the hard city pavement, their hats flying from their heads. In school I was beginning to be subject to suffocating anxiety when I was placed in the middle of a group. It seemed so easy to simply forget how to breathe; so easy to feel sick; so easy to feel a desperate need to get out. When I was singing in chorus or playing clarinet in the school orchestra, I couldn't wait until these activities would end and I could go back to feeling human. In fourth grade, standing in a group reciting a passage from Exodus, I felt my face grow ice cold and I fainted dead away. These experiences marked the beginning of what turned into my lifelong struggle with agoraphobia, but at the time I didn't have a word for them. Apart from the embarrassingly public fainting episode, no one knew about them.

When I was nine, my parents, normally overly protective, took me with them to see Ingmar Bergman's new film *Wild Strawberries*. The frightening opening sequence, in which Victor Sjöström's character has a nightmare, hit me like a cannonball in the stomach. In the old doctor's dream he finds himself walking down a deserted village street and comes to a clock with no hands on it. At the next corner he sees a figure in a dark hat and coat facing away from him. When he approaches the figure and taps him on the shoulder, the face that turns toward him is like an empty sandbag, and the entire body collapses to the sidewalk like a dummy, with a sickening squooshing sound. A riderless horse then approaches, carrying a wagon with a coffin on it. The wagon wheel catches on a lamppost and jerks forward and back, causing the coffin to rock and make a creaking sound like a baby's cry. Finally the wheel breaks free and clatters down the street as the horse scampers away, while the coffin falls at the doctor's feet and its lid cracks apart just enough for the hand of the corpse inside to fall out. Drawn to this dangling arm, the doctor finds his hand suddenly seized by the hand of the corpse, and he engages in a mortal struggle. Finally the lid falls open completely, and the doctor stares into his own dead face in the coffin. I was terrified even by the clock with no hands, but when the hollow-eyed potato sack of a man crumpled to the ground, I shot up into the air from my seat.

In summers I became more aware of being part of a cultural subset—people of Jewish ancestry—who weren't always welcome. It is hard to know where this inkling started. I already knew enough about the Holocaust for it to figure in my nightmares and frightening fantasies. I remember that my brother told me that our parents were rumored to be the first Jews who had ever rented a house in Bronxville, and that no Jews owned houses there.

Camp Mohawk taught me the names of Native American tribes but nothing about Native Americans. Some dim connection formed in my mind between the fact that we non–Native Americans were referring to ourselves as "Iroquois," "Onondagas," and "Cayugas" at the camp and the scarcity of Jews in Bronxville. Mohawk introduced me to a kind of herd mentality for the first time. I had never had to pledge allegiance to the American flag before. In our family little flags were trotted out for July Fourth, a holiday that seemed to move our parents, the way the words of Lincoln, Roosevelt, and Adlai Stevenson did, or the excited mayhem of the Democratic convention, or documentaries about World War II. But being told to stand at attention, put one hand over the heart, and recite a specific patriotic pledge felt coercive and alien. An enforced mantra dedicating one to "liberty" seemed self-contradictory. And if the point were really liberty and justice "for all," how come we were wearing the names of former Native American tribes on our T-shirts?

Since activities at Mohawk were largely athletic, I was also particularly conscious of being in another minority: that of short people. I tried to compensate with my intellectual side. Counselors joked with me about the fact that I was always reading. Mohawk tried to instill in us a sense of realism and toughness in relation to nature. We learned the names of butterflies and how to catch them in green butterfly nets, kill them with a pinch of formaldehyde from little droppers, and pin them to mats made of cork. During one nature class we watched as a boa constrictor ate a live mouse whole. At the moment when the mouse's hind portion was sticking out of the snake's head, with its little back feet still wriggling, I bolted and headed back to our cabin, grabbed a book, and lay down on my blanket.

Like all "shrimps" everywhere, I was roughed up from time to time at camp. On a couple of occasions I got into fights with groups of bigger boys when I came to the defense of retarded and Down syndrome campers. Obviously, I made the connection to Mary in my own mind, even if few of my friends even knew that I was a twin. I may even have dimly wondered what it would have been like to have Mary at the camp there with me, or why it was that there were at least some mentally handicapped children who did live with their parents. My nemesis at the camp was a tall cocky boy who liked to be a bully. At home my father had told me that the boy's father was a noted Mafia figure. One day this boy pushed one of the retarded campers and made him cry, and I got into a furious fistfight with him, in which I was far outmatched. Lying in the grass reduced to tears myself, I yelled at him in my loudest possible voice, "Your father is a gangster!" at which point he looked absolutely shocked, and even backed away, stung by my words. The meaning of the moment instantly changed, and I suddenly felt guilty, as if I myself had become the bully.

Meanwhile, away at Sandpiper, Mary was showing encouraging

growth. Under Miss Anderson's tutelage she greatly expanded her arithmetic skills and advanced well into the primary school level and somewhat beyond. She filled out endless pages of workbooks of addition, subtraction, multiplication, and division problems and eventually even some early work on fractions. She sat in drawing classes and carefully copied schematic houses, flowers, trees, and the sun, in prescribed colors. Some of these were used as cards. She wrote slowly and neatly in ruled notebooks, eventually moving from block printing to a solid cursive, practiced on paper in which each solid black line was bisected by a thin stripe of light blue dashes to help the students center each letter. Amazingly, she learned to read, at least at the level of a third or fourth grader. Even more amazingly, she learned to read music. She took regular piano lessons and performed in little recitals at the house. She also seemed to have a genuine friendship with her roommate, a red-haired girl named Josie. Mary became more ladylike in her years at Sandpiper, developing into a young woman who looked, if anything, more "normal" than ever.

She was taken regularly to church, where she sometimes played the piano for hymns. From the beginning Miss Anderson simply treated her as a fellow Protestant—presumably because it was convenient and natural to bring her along to the local church services she and the other children attended—and since Mary seemed to enjoy the outings into town and benefit from the chance to play the piano there, my parents didn't object. I assume that Miss Anderson understood that we were Jewish by ancestry. Mary still knows how to play "Onward Christian Soldiers," and her medical records still list her as "Protestant."

At Sandpiper she had an optimal level of supervision but also a kind of freedom she never could have had in New York. The lovely clapboard house overlooked the water but was sufficiently fenced in to permit the children to run outside and play unchaperoned on the swings and jungle gyms. Mary particularly loved the swings. Even after the first summer had passed, the school maintained a happy, almost carefree air, as if on vacation from standard expectations. The house was filled with light, and the air from the Atlantic was salty and briny. The voices of the children were animated and sometimes unusual. One boy wore a hearing aid and spoke in a pleading, nasal, somewhat garbled tone. Often many voices were raised at once.

Miss Anderson was intelligent, intrepid—an original. Her face struck me as furry and manly; her hair was always slightly unkempt; she had the appearance of someone in the trenches who was totally oblivious to her own appearance, far removed from the urban world of glamour and adult banter. My parents seemed to view her almost as if she were a nun—sexless and selfless—and I unthinkingly absorbed this view of her too.

Family visits to Sandpiper were momentous for me. For a brief moment we were reconstituted as a family of five, but in an alien context and surrounded by strangers. We ate tuna fish sandwiches with the children at one of the shiny wooden tables in the combined dining room–kitchen and watched as they did their chores of cleaning up and washing the dishes. Sometimes a child would get upset, cry, or complain in a strange whiny voice. Sometimes an older child would go and sit on one of the teachers' laps, as if he were still a four-year-old.

Trips to see Mary and to visit the schools my brother and I attended were the only true vacation we ever took as a family. (After all, when we were in Bronxville, our father returned to New York every weekday to work.) In order to get to Chatham my parents would hire a limousine and driver (or perhaps, in fact, the magazine paid for this). Both my brother and I were discomfited by the lack of intimacy this imposed, and mortified by the impression it gave of family wealth. We arrived in a vehicle fit for royalty—or so it seemed to me then—and once there I rarely had a moment alone with Mary, or even had a chance to realize that I wished to have one.

Whether because of instinctively sensing the shrillness in my mother's assertions of family togetherness, or because of the loss of Mary in our daily routine, I started becoming almost obsessively concerned with the idea of truthfulness, with locating a firm basis beneath everything that was being said around me. I became aware that our last name was misleadingly Irish-sounding, that we celebrated Christian holidays despite our Jewish ancestry. The limousine seemed one more instance of a false appearance. In addition to not being truly wealthy ourselves, we descended from people of humble means. In that era, traveling by limousine instantly conveyed a message of complacent affluence, perhaps of money going back generations. I found the distance between that message and the way I saw myself jarring. Trivial as the distinction may actually be, I was already touchy enough about my privileged childhood without having the extent of its advantages exaggerated.

However, trips out to the Cape were indeed preceded by a night of glittering sumptuousness in Boston, where we stayed at the Ritz-Carlton, across from Boston Common and the Swan Boats. At night we had dinner in the dining room, where I ordered lamb chops and my brother, lobster and oysters, and we drank Shirley Temples. We sometimes went to musicals in pre-Broadway previews (*Mr. President*; *On a Clear Day You Can See Forever*) or to a jazz club. My brother and I shared a plush bedroom adjoining that of our parents'. The memory of such enjoyable extravagance seems almost unreal to me today.

The visits to Mary stirred a mystifying mix of emotions, at the bottom of which was intense sadness. Folded into this was the tension traveling caused our parents, which somehow adhered to all their travel routines: the stops at the side of the highway for my father to call the magazine or, unbeknownst to me then, his second family, from a pay phone; my mother's obsessive consulting of the map showing the way; the manuscripts being read and edited in the car.

When we would arrive, Mary would usually be dressed in a skirt or sweater that my mother had bought. She would come over to us and say all of our names; she would accept our hugs; she might take our mother's hand, or our father's hand, or mine, or my brother's, and walk us over to a place to sit down. But essentially this would all be done in one motion, as she primarily focused on the shopping bag of presents that she was so eager to open. She might narrate the features of the event-in-progress—"Mary Shawn's parents are coming"; "Mary has presents"; "chicken salad, iced tea, ice cream, and cake, peanut butter cups for dessert"—and she would sometimes laugh looking at us ("Hi, Allen"), as if in recognition that we were actually in fact there. "Wallace came for a visit." "Mommy brought presents." "Wallace, Mary, and Allen will have ice cream and cake." All in all, there was no comparison between the way she had seemed in New York and the way she appeared to be here. She looked wonderfully well. One almost could imagine seeing on her face that she was with people who had a way of understanding her.

Mary was still slightly taller than me. In this respect, and also because she had been sent "away to school," there was reason for me to feel that I was still the baby of the family, which, having been born five minutes after Mary, technically I was.

In retrospect I see my parents as having been in radically different gears during these visits. My father, agoraphobic, bundled in his overcoat as he tended to be in most seasons, and surely was when near the ocean, was vulnerable so far from New York and, still further out on a limb, far from Boston, deeply emotional about seeing Mary, moved by the plight of the children at the school and by its idyllic and to him exotic locale, must have felt almost overwhelmed by the effort of the trip, the poignancy of the family story, and the burden of the decisions they had made and would continue to have to make about Mary. My mother, who formed extraordinarily personal attachments with everyone connected to the family, was engaged and active, carrying packages for Mary, intent on having a conference with Miss Anderson, visiting Mary's room, chatting with Josie—Mary's roommate—asking if the winter clothes she had mailed Mary fit her.

In one blurry picture taken during a summer visit, I am wearing a camera around my neck. Another is one I probably took myself: my mother and Mary on adjoining swings, with Mary leaning over to kiss my mother's cheek.

The mood of the return trip was always deeply different, as if we had been cleansed somehow: a kind of wasted, tender exhaustion and calm. On the way home we always talked about Mary and about little else, and my mother invariably said that Mary had seemed so much better, that she had spoken more, or seemed calmer, or more grown up, or for the first time had done something she had never done before. For several years at Chatham, this was actually true. Once my father put it this way: "She's happier than we are."

The physical relaxation of the return ride—the downhill coast of it—was palpable. Sometimes my father took out his work from his briefcase again but ended up just holding it in his lap the whole way. Reduced by fatigue, relief, sadness, and gratification to an elemental state of family togetherness, we still did not say exactly what was on our minds. It was still not possible to give vent to a sense of grief or discouragement. Sometimes I would strike a sour note, disputing that Mary was improving, or questioning whether she was being treated well, but these types of comments went beyond the reach of what our family talks could bear. However deep the emotions were that we shared nonverbally, our discussions about Mary in the car on the return trip were themselves rituals with certain rules.

Once home we did not talk further about Mary. There might be one more conversation the following day, one last cloud drifting by from the overcast sky of the day before, but then the matter would be closed again.

I never knew if Mary suffered when she was left at Sandpiper after that first summer. When I try to imagine now how she might have reacted to being told that she was staying, or how she was prepared for that, I cannot. Our mother used to tell us that she was happy to stay and that she was in fact afraid not of remaining there, but of returning to New York, that when she was taken on any excursion she needed to be reassured that it wouldn't take her back home ("Not to New York! Not to New York!"). She may well have been right. Mary certainly was better *understood* in that environment than in her own home. Our mother speculated that even seeing the apartment on Ninety-sixth Street again would frighten Mary into thinking she was returning there for good. Many, many years later, when our mother could no longer visit Mary herself, we took this admonition to heart and made sure that even in New York we brought Mary to a neutral place—a rented room in a hotel—for our brief birthday lunches with her.

Years into Mary's life at Sandpiper, when she and I were fourteen or fifteen, I asked my parents if I could spend the summer months at Sandpiper, perhaps getting a job there. This was discouraged, with the argument that, like a visit to the apartment, my presence could stir confusion and sadness in Mary, causing her at the very least to become overly attached to me.

5

THINGS NOT SEEN

Perhaps it was just coincidental, but in Mary's absence I became instinctively interested in the intangible sides of life, in invisible things. Pursuing my interest in dreams, I managed to get my parents and many of their friends to tell me examples of theirs for a school paper I did on the subject. One of our teachers astutely gave us the assignment to visit both a Protestant and a Catholic church and to write up our responses. I fell in love with the Catholic service. For a while I attended Mass with some regularity. Once again, as I had with my "television show," I found release in a solitary activity through which I nevertheless felt a sense of human connectedness. The congregation at the church I attended was Hispanic, mostly poor, and often elderly. The Mass was in Latin, a text I knew from music. There was a stone representation of the crucifixion, and a monument to the virgin who happened to have the same name as my sister. The space was cavernous, cold, echoing, and rarely terribly full. The priest's voice unfurled in the air in a murmuring singsong; there were bells and chimes of various registers, the sounds of rustling coats when people rose and were seated, and of mumbled prayers ringing against the statuary. I said the prayers; I knelt; I participated—as an outsider, but in my mind as a kind of guest participant. This was the extent of my brief Catholic phase. Entering a religious space made sense to me, even bowing down and "worshipping" made sense to me— even though specific religious beliefs made no sense to me at all. The idea of a religious space, the need to find a place where religious feeling is expressed, has stayed with me. In fact, I'd hesitate to call myself a nonbeliever, because I find the question of whether one believes absurd, even irritating. Life is infinitely wondrous, infinitely cruel, and incomprehensible. What is there to believe or not to believe?

My interest in religion eventually carried over to other school projects, such as our study of the Reformation, in which we read John Osborne's play about Martin Luther and Erik Erikson's analytic biography of him. I memorized much of Paul's letter to the Corinthians (without, of course, knowing that Saint Paul was a former Jew who, like my father, had changed his name). In my wallet I carried a picture of Martin Luther King Jr., in between one of my friend Jay and one of Willie Mays making an over-the-shoulder catch.

Drawing, too, was an outlet everywhere and at all times of day. At home any spare piece of paper or pad could become the background for a person's face. Half the faces I drew were of African Americans. The rest were father figures, complete with fedora, suit, and tie; assorted ministers and priests; and curvaceous women, even though depicting their curves required a degree of talent and knowledge of anatomy I didn't have.

———

The summer Mary went away to camp is not one I remember well. I only know that in her absence music seemed different to me. When I was four or five, music teachers had noticed that I could keep a beat, and I had started participating in my father's pianistic jam sessions by playing along on a child's leather-skinned tom-tom with a picture of an "American Indian" chieftain on it. Before long I was playing on a snare drum and cymbal with brushes. Eventually I acquired a high-hat. In truth, my drum playing had never been terribly good. I learned the rudiments of reading rhythms and the treble clef through recorder lessons at age eight, and soon began learning clarinet. But I was actually much more interested in my brother's violin. In fact I committed one of my childhood crimes because I longed for a toy violin I saw in a store window on Madison Avenue a few blocks from home. The violin cost a peculiar amount (something like $9.78), far beyond anything I could save from my weekly allowance, and my request for it was fruitless, since it was not holiday season. As it happened, my brother was not exactly compulsively neat with his belongings, and this included the spare change he removed from his windbreaker pocket, which, along with wads of Kleenex and copies of *MAD* magazine, lay scattered on his desk. Knowing that what I was doing was reprehensible, I snuck into his room and removed exactly the change I needed from the surface of his desk, walked down the block, and made my purchase. When my mother saw me with the violin she was instantly suspicious, and her expression made my heart sink. I claimed that, to my amazement, I had found just the right amount of change lying on the sidewalk in front of our apartment building. But before I completed my explanation I burst into tears with shame and remorse. The toy violin was returned to the store.

The first time music reached me in a new way after Mary left home was at a performance of *Swan Lake* at the City Center on Fifty-sixth Street. It must have been Balanchine's truncated version with its tragic ending. Instead of being reunited with Odette in human form at the ballet's close, the Prince watched his beloved disappear forever, still under her spell as a swan. Tchaikovsky's surgingly emotional music started some internal mechanism within me. After that, while I still enjoyed drawing, and baseball, and being funny, and writing stories, I now found myself preoccupied with music, in some way, all day long. Inspired by my father's piano playing, I began to spend time at the keyboard trying to learn the passages from *Rhapsody in Blue* I remembered, and then finding chords and tunes of my own to play. It came naturally to make things up, extend them, and memorize them. My notational skills were too limited for me to write these "pieces" down. I didn't even yet know how to write in the bass clef. But I gave the music titles ("The Dying Accordion Player" was one), and at a memorable school assembly when I was in fourth grade, in front of two hundred middle school students, I sat down at the piano and performed a few of them. I remember so well this first time experiencing the thrill of being applauded not just politely but with excitement; the sudden rush of feeling special; this breakthrough of unencumbered, wholehearted expression—escape from myself, from my family, from my chronological age, from my anxieties— into the freedom of sounds.

Music belonged to me. Somehow I could be fully alive in music in a way I never had been before. I disappeared inside it yet discovered a new self there. Tones could be combined to speak in a powerful way, as powerfully as necessary, but I could still remain protected.

I had not had piano lessons yet, but my love of the instrument and these musical inventions of mine persuaded my parents to find me a teacher. They seemed almost stunned by this development.

My emergence as a little musician brought me attention at school and in the family in a new way. My piano teacher, Frances Dillon, had a belief in my talent and took me seriously as a future composer, swiftly propelling me over the hurdle of learning notation. In the seventh grade I appeared in a school production of *The Tempest* as Ariel (my friend Jay was Caliban) and got to write and sing my own songs to Shakespeare's beautiful verses, also finally putting my recorder playing to good use. It wasn't long before I was asked to write a piece for the school orchestra, and it also wasn't long before I heard the word "genius" used about me by my classmates and teachers. They didn't mean any harm, yet strangely the word actually hurt. There aren't as many child composers as there are child painters, writers, or actors, and the presence of one creates a kind of giddiness. For my parents, who had suffered from the curse cast over their daughter—compelling her to remain a swan despite her humanity—how tempting it must have been to think that, as if in compensation, a lucky spell had been cast on me.

Miss Dillon's lessons were never routine. Her sense of music was dynamic and extraordinarily alive. She had a habit of pacing around the room while one played—for example, shouting over Beethoven's music, "What a composer!" or "Listen to the left hand!" or "Into the keys . . . and suffer!" She was just what I needed in my life, not only someone to encourage me and believe in me, but also an adult who was less inhibited and proper than my parents. Along with lessons held in the bustling atmosphere of Mannes College on Seventy-fourth Street, we met many Saturdays at her apartment just off Lexington Avenue, where she would sit next to me in her silk Chinese bathrobe, with her cat, Pita, asleep next to the piano pedals, and lessons could take as much time as necessary. Although she clearly had confidence in me as a budding composer, she probably wished that I would decide to be a pianist instead. She had me play Chopin, Berg, and Prokofiev for her college pedagogy classes. She seemed to value my aesthetic instincts. Together, with her playing the orchestra reduction, we played through Bach's D Minor Concerto and Mozart's C Minor Concerto, K. 491. In a report to my parents I read years later, she wrote that my playing was "on a high college level." I was fourteen.

Even though Miss Dillon probably understood me in a way that no one else did, I did not confide in her my feelings of anxiety and claustrophobia, feelings that surely steered me away from the ambition to be a performer. She knew that I suffered from stomachaches and that I had spent more than a few days lying on my side in pain on the cold octagonal tiles of my bathroom floor. In allowing me to learn to play Alban Berg's Sonata, op. 1, the work of a hypersensitive twenty-one-year-old who had attempted suicide, she surely understood that it would be an outlet for an important side of my personality. Berg's explicit despair and controlled hysteria struck a chord with me, and I memorized the work easily. It was one of the few pieces I played without nervousness, because, I suppose, it gave vent to the rage and agitation I normally tried to suppress in public.

During this time I was introduced by Miss Dillon and by concerts, visits to nightclubs, recordings, and television broadcasts to a wide range of musical idioms. Bowled over by Bartók, Stravinsky, Schoenberg, Berg, Ives, Prokofiev, Ellington, Mingus, and Thelonious Monk, I was aroused to a sense of purpose as a future composer. Music from the more distant past—Bach, Mozart,

Beethoven—seemed breathtaking the way a mountain view was, but more a permanent part of nature itself than something I could incorporate into my own way of being a composer. Many of these introductions happened through my brother, who, notwithstanding any jealousy he might have felt about what was happening to me, sat with me in our living room listening to music. In this way we heard Schoenberg's *Moses und Aron*, with its opening lines ("... one, infinite, omnipresent, unperceived and inconceivable ...") that could have stood for several aspects of our family life, and Berg's operas *Wozzeck* and *Lulu*, and we followed the scores to Bach's *Saint Matthew Passion* and Beethoven's late string quartets, music from the past that I loved as much as any twentieth-century music. My brother also played the innumerable pieces I wrote for him on solo violin and for the two of us on violin and piano, and— indispensably for my later life—worked with me on our puppet shows, for which he wrote the words and I now wrote the music. He even copied out some of my music by hand.

My brother was already admired for his intelligence and strong personality, for being a thinker and a born performer, a ham who was also brilliant and deeply serious. Full of sociable zest, he had always been a natural focus of attention. I still remember my feeling of pride when I was excused from class at the age of five so that I could sit in the school auditorium and watch him playing the role of Socrates in a school play. It was typecasting. By the time I began to compose, he had already achieved some notoriety for the frankness of his short stories, which pushed at the boundaries of reticence and taste exemplified by our father's magazine, and whose subject matter caused a few of his more demure teachers to be scandalized. Even his childhood paintings had drawn fire. His one-man show in the Dalton School lobby—the school was at that time without equal in giving its students solo opportunities to shine—had led some teachers to call for the removal of the paintings deemed too violent or sensual for an elementary school exhibit. But just as importantly, his use of language was already fluidly, floridly virtuosic, and had always been naturally so. He had a musician's ear for speech even at age eight, when he wrote this Mother's Day card:

Here's to the finest most motherly mother God ever put on this earth.

Even in his early teens, his writing was infused with a lush sensuousness far from the restrained family ethos—full of bodily appetites and excretions, and closer to South American magical realism, or to the style of Norman Mailer, than to the urbane understatement of a John Cheever, William Maxwell, or many of the writers our father published. At home my parents applauded his intellectual vitality and his high-minded, rational side—a family friend predicted that someday he might be a judge—but seemed wary of his imagination and literary powers.

Having presumably craved attention (beyond that of my imaginary television audience), I was certainly getting it for my musical efforts. At the same time, I knew perfectly well that I wasn't a real composer yet. It was confusing to go from the enveloping privacy and concentration of trying to get the notes right to the public sphere in which my parents and others voiced indiscriminate, exaggerated enthusiasm about what I had written. To me the music was something I was working on; to others it was magic. It was also not lost on me that while I had quickly been labeled a "gifted artist," my brother, who was already nearly a mature one, was prized only for his verbal "skills" and "logical mind." We were both being pigeonholed.

In one respect my brother was fortunate that his artistic work was considered scandalous. It had the effect of keeping his literary work private. By contrast, my music was considered a kind of delicate public plant that needed just the right kind of soil, sunshine, and watering. Clearly this had everything to do with Mary's delicacy and the fears bequeathed to me as the twin with a viable future in society. But the attention made me want to go back into hiding.

My father's interest in jazz and our frequent nighttime excursions to clubs exerted a huge influence on me, but my mother viewed the life of jazz musicians and the sexy, ecstatic, transgressive ethos of the music with trepidation. In truth, both my parents cherished a view of my future as amounting to some kind of settled and achieved eminence, and were uncomfortable with the precariousness and unpredictability of actual artists' lives. My father lived within a world of enormous accomplishment, and with people whose work had already succeeded, or which he was in a position to foster. His own experience of being an individual artist, in both music and writing, had not progressed far beyond the journeyman stage, and had left him with unfulfilled longings and perhaps doubts about whether he could have faced worldly failure or truly plumbed his own complex nature. His fear seemed to attach itself to the very style and content of my brother's early writing. In my case, it seemed to express itself as a conviction that whatever I did would succeed. When I played the piano he said that I sounded "like Richter"; when I conducted I looked "like Bernstein"— comparisons that, supportive as they were, made me ashamed by being so out of scale to the potential I felt in myself, and worried that only the loftiest level of achievement would count for him. We frequently went to dinner at a restaurant where an aging cocktail pianist played tastefully tinkling accompaniments, and my parents worried aloud in a joking way about my ending up doing that. For me it was not a particularly funny joke, as I could hear how skillful the pianist in fact was, and perhaps even then sensed that I would be taking on many similar jobs in my life. (And today I know that it was a perfectly good job to have.)

My mother, for her part, took it upon herself to chaperone my listening habits, instituting a rule that I could listen to only one jazz record for every three classical ones. This seemed to place upon my own shoulders a conflict between my parents' views of music, and stimulated more conflict in me. Having instinctively used the abstraction of music to express myself unguardedly and finally break out of my circumscribed role as the "easy" child, I now saw that even music could be considered "badly behaved." My mother was also at times suspicious of Miss Dillon, thinking her overly possessive, and sometimes complaining that she was "crude."

Like many young composers I was galvanized by my first encounter with Stravinsky's *Le Sacre du Printemps*, heard on a recording seated next to Miss Dillon in Bronxville. Here was an eruption as primal as those that rocked Mary, a universal outcry ripping through the fabric of propriety, joyful and tragic simultaneously. *Le Sacre* seemed to rage at the finitude of life while transcending it. Its catharsis was abstract, nonverbal, "primitive" in affect, yet also deeply elegant. A few months later I attended a performance by the Juilliard Quartet of Bartók's Sixth String Quartet, his last, the one in which the same doleful theme introduces the first three movements and then dominates the fourth, and when I came home I told my parents that I now knew I wanted to be a composer. The Bartók for me represented a kind of stealth attack on the self-restraint demanded by civilized life. It seemed to speak unguardedly of death and anguish, but in a public language and with a sense of decorum that could be tolerated. These musical encounters occurred during the same year that Miss Dillon allowed me to study Berg's op. 1 Sonata and assigned Schoenberg's exquisite *Six Little Pieces* (*Sechs kleine Stücke*). These four dark twentieth-century works marked me for life.

When it came time to compose for the middle school orchestra in the spring of my thirteenth year, I first sketched out some violent passages full of rhythmic dislocations and dissonant harmonies no doubt inspired by Stravinsky. The excited look on the face of the music teacher when I showed him the sketches ameliorated the discouragement I felt when he told me that I had to be more realistic and practical when writing for a school ensemble. Putting these pages aside, then, I decided to take a piano piece I had written for and "about" my brother and turn it into a piece for piano and orchestra. "Older Brother," as it was called, was a theme and variations based on the traditional singsong taunt of children. The variations explored various moods and styles, ranging from the lushly lyrical to a jazz episode in which I played directly on the lower strings of the piano with soft mallets, creating a quasi–double bass effect. The work's title could just as easily have been "Younger Brother," since it was a portrait of my own affectionate and teasing hero worship of my brother. Juvenile as this effort undoubtedly was, it gave me an instant education in form, orchestration, and project completion. Thinking back on it now, I see that Mary was in the piece too, that the fact that the programmatic content of this first large-scale piece was about a sibling was not by chance. Music was a language my sister had understood before I had. Music was helping me to feel connected to her and to give voice to the many contradictory emotions being her brother and losing her companionship had left me with. It is also tempting to think that if "Older Brother" was about my brother, my original, violent sketches had been about Mary. And like her they had been "discarded" as being too unruly and wild.

At the same time that I appeared to be musically forging ahead, I was keenly aware of my deficiencies. I composed with the same spontaneity with which I drew faces, often sitting on my bed sketching out a score, which somehow I found I could hear in my head. (Miss Dillon told my parents that I had perfect pitch.) Yet I didn't know anything about formal composition. When I listened back to a completed piece, I felt that my music had remained a sketch—with a good overall form, an emotional purpose, and many nice touches—but also with gaps in continuity, thin patches, and, occasionally, real blunders. I wasn't ashamed of the music, only of being already called a "composer." Like my reaction to traveling by limousine, I was painfully self-conscious about the disparity between the way things looked to others and the way they really seemed to me.

I was also just plain afraid. When my clarinet teacher suggested that his woodwind quintet might play the quintet I had written, I procrastinated about handing him the piece until he had forgotten about the idea. Through my friend Hank, whose family was close to Leonard Bernstein, I got the opportunity to sing in the boys' choir section of Mahler's Third Symphony with the New York Philharmonic. I turned down the offer, fearing I would be overwhelmed by claustrophobia onstage.

Unbeknownst to me, in the audience at my middle school orchestra performance were Mr. and Mrs. David Dushkin, directors of Kinhaven Music Camp in Weston, Vermont. The camp had been recommended to my parents, and my mother had written the Dushkins about my upcoming musical performance, which happened to coincide with their annual visit to New York to audition young people. Evidently my composition, in which I also played the piano part, was my audition, and apparently I passed. Seeing the Dushkins in their overcoats in the school auditorium I had the impression of a magical pair, radiating a lifetime of involvement in both music and education. I learned later that the Dushkins had met as students of Nadia Boulanger in Paris, where they had both studied to be composers. David, the camp director, was elegant and warm, the very soul of gentle sanity. He was born in Russia and was the brother of Samuel Dushkin, with whom Stravinsky toured America giving duo recitals, and for whom he wrote his Violin Concerto. Dorothy was a member of a distinguished New England family. Flinty, playful, and vigorous by nature, it was she who had remained a composer. When she wasn't working on music, she was working in her garden in her floppy hat and muddy boots, weeding and pruning and stopping to mop her brow.

Kinhaven, where I spent the next four summers, was as close to paradise as I am likely to get. Situated in a verdant, gloriously mountainous region of Vermont, it was ringed by lush hillsides over which floated the most fascinating cottony cumulus clouds I have ever seen. We were surrounded by nature and by music all day long. I played clarinet and piano in chamber groups and was encouraged to compose. In my first summer I wrote a wind quintet and again tried my hand at writing for orchestra, this time for a group that included a full brass section and had double basses in the string section. I would sit under a tree, barefoot, working on the music, with the sounds of rustling leaves, distant shouts of campers swimming or playing volleyball, or someone practicing the French horn, in my ears. My orchestra piece was called *Overture to a Ballgame*. In it I used the opening few notes from "Take Me Out to the Ball Game" as a musical motive, and illustrated imaginary baseball situations in an impressionistic way, with the crack of a woodblock standing for the sound of a bat. Like a ball game, the piece had its moments of suspense, uproar, and drift—as well as a certain nostalgic tenderness. Mr. Dushkin asked me to conduct it at the final summer concerts when the parents came to pick up their children. A week before the concert I came down with a sore throat, a stiff neck, a savage headache, and a high fever. I felt not just sick but as if I would never be well again. Mr. Dushkin himself watched over my care in the infirmary, treating me not just like a camper but like a "sick artist," often personally bringing me pills and juice in little paper cups, looking like a concerned World War I medic tending the dying. By the day of the concert I had revived enough to shakily mount the podium and conduct. When the music was playing, I felt split in two. On the one hand, I felt almost preternaturally vigorous and optimistic; on the other hand, I felt as if a terrible illness was trying to drag me down into an early grave.

This same pattern repeated itself every summer I was at the camp: I would compose my orchestra piece, fall into a serious fever, and revive just in time to conduct it. It is hard for me not to remember this in almost mythic terms, as some kind of violent altercation between my outer and inner selves, as if a part of me were trying to bring the emotions and unknowable inner life of Mary back from the underworld, and with her to finally expose to light my own deepest feelings. Apparently it was one thing to achieve these assertions of the life force on paper, and another to stand up and identify them as my own in public.

6

CRACKS BETWEEN
THE KEYS

For four years running, starting when I was in sixth grade, I was like an only child in my parents' apartment. Apart from vacations, my brother was away at school, first at the Putney School, a progressive school on a farm in Vermont, and then at Harvard, while his room remained a museum of his preoccupations until he was fourteen. Whenever he returned, he had always changed again, animated by new acquaintances, interests, and stories, and eager to keep me up-to-date on them. The subject matter of our annual Christmas puppet shows (which continued until I was nineteen and my brother twenty-four) charted his intellectual evolution and challenged me to adapt my musical idiom to each theme and locale. By the time he was in college we were doing shows about ancient China and the Odes of Horace. In his absence, which lasted most of the year, the household felt demagnetized. Mary's absence was like a deep cave that had been excavated in her bedroom but remained unmentioned. Meanwhile I grew closer to my mother and unknowingly sensed her fears for her marriage and her fears of letting go of me.

The family arguments that would sometimes erupt over the holidays tended to originate in a test of wills between my brother and my parents over whether I could accompany him to this or that "sophisticated" party or on some dangerous or "overstimulating" outing. Having early on tested the limits of artistic propriety, my brother also strained against parental restrictions, admonitions, and fears. My mother worried that I was attracted to my brother's girlfriends and that one of them might sneak into bed with me, something that, unfortunately, never happened. I was dimly aware that while my brother had managed to separate himself from the family stylistically, philosophically, and physically, some dread surrounded my own maturing process. In a private moment during this time, my mother once quietly said to me, "I know you won't rebel the way your brother has."

In these years as an "only child," I was unknowingly marinating in the conflict between my parents over my father's secret love life, and I was surrounded at every moment by reminders of my sister, without the presence of my brother's strong personality to dispel a sense of sadness that had settled over the house.

In my first year of high school, spent in New York attending Friends Seminary on East Sixteenth Street, I was the opposite of an agoraphobic. I came home from school every night and actually begged my parents to allow me to go away to school the following year in Vermont, as my brother had at the same age. I could sense that my parents were clinging to me and hoped that I would remain with them in the apartment for longer than my brother had. I never once thought of it from their point of view, or even considered that I was their last child to leave. At Friends I felt like an outsider and became a member of what one might call a "negative subculture," a group of slouching misfits, linked more by a dislike of the school than by mutual affection. It was also where I encountered the adversarial style of teaching for the first time: the English teacher who taught the difference between "its" and "it's" by marking any essay that confused the two as an F and then drawing a red line from the offending usage straight through to the end of the paper; the pinched, repressed, epicene music teacher who blushed to the roots of his hair trying to browbeat us into injecting vitality into the dreary four-part arrangement of "On the Street Where You Live" we were forced to sing. The school seemed to foster a sense of upbeat conformity in the rest of the student body; students smiled falsely walking down the halls, unctuously flattering teachers. The teacher I liked best, Mrs. T, conveyed some true complexity. Students whispered that she was divorced. It became clear to me that she was a music lover when the "Dies Irae" from Verdi's *Requiem* began playing in a distant classroom, and she paused to thrill to the sound of its anguished chorus and primal bass drum thwacks. I found the communality of Quaker meetings false and remained unmoved by the spontaneously inspirational comments students and faculty rose to offer. I did appreciate the silences. In them I contemplated my escape from the school and the exciting possibilities lying in wait in the future.

My happiest moments were the lunch breaks when I could improvise at the piano in the meeting hall for forty-five minutes. It didn't bother me or distract me that a number of students would bring their lunch into the hall while I played. Another happy memory is of performing Bartók's *Three Rondos* at a concert in the hall. But the year passed primarily in strain and awkwardness. Friends was like a pinching shoe that simply did not fit me.

———

In my second summer at Kinhaven I again found myself in paradise, again composed an orchestra piece, again was sick for a week before the performance, and again rose from my bed to conduct it. This was also the summer I found love, in the person of a small and delicate young violinist and singer with curly blond hair, who looked like a Fra Angelico angel. While I had already had a string of unrequited infatuations—the previous summer I had glued myself to a doe-eyed flutist who wanted only friendship from me—this time I had fixed on someone who reciprocated. A literate, poetic girl with a quiet wit and a passionate inner life, L had tiny, perfect features and a quiet, melodious voice like the tinkling of little bells. Starting with our common small stature, in every way she and I were plausible together. We shared a sensual, somewhat ironic nature hidden behind an innocent-looking exterior. However, there were times when, next to her extreme refinement, I felt almost boorish. I thought that I didn't deserve her, that she admired me too much. But if there was a serious problem between us, it was simply that I had a twin sister whom I tended not to think about. I didn't recognize that, having come into the world coupled to Mary, for me love was a return. When I took L's hand, I knew we were in love, but I didn't know why holding her hand felt so strangely familiar.

In addition, my brother and I had, in our very different ways, soaked up the contradictory sexual messages of our household: our mother's overflowing romantic feeling for our father, contrasted with her nervous, cautionary words about sex; our father's aura of passions suppressed and rarely expressed openly. While our mother seemed fixated on their first twenty-five years together—the years of their courtship, honeymoon, struggling times in the 1930s in New York, and the birth of their first child, my brother—our father made few comments about their marriage and rarely invoked his, or their, past. There was a primness to the way he kissed her goodbye on the way out the door to work, or about the way he accepted her hand when she reached for his, that could have been taken for shyness, discretion, detachment from his romantic feelings for her, or squeamishness about sex itself—it was impossible to tell which. On the other hand he visibly relished the physical presence and appearance of other women he knew or saw in movies or on television, and, at least within the family, wouldn't hesitate to comment on their attractiveness. Our mother's bureau was full of the little love notes he wrote to her throughout their marriage. Yet some writers at the magazine seemed to think he was a monk. There was a joke about the fact that his children were proof he had "done it twice."

The magazine itself, of course, was famously euphemistic in its use of language pertaining to acts of the body. And this tactfulness extended not only to sex but, to a degree, to all the messier aspects of life, except those of a global and political significance. Divorces, addictions, medical and psychological problems were not the stuff of profiles, and as themes were handled discreetly even in fiction.

Meanwhile the unseen sides of our family's life—our sister's disability and absence, our parents' psychological and marital struggles—were probably fueling my brother's and my creative efforts, since precisely those aspects of life that seemed generally absent from family talk and from the magazine—the tasteless, the lurid, the unreasonable, the violent, the uncontrollable, the personal, the psychological—seemed most fascinating. Several of my brother's puppet show plots revolved around secret lives. In one, "Fins and Feet," a psychiatrist had a secret life in the ocean, where he was able to talk to dolphins and, at the same time, unbeknownst to his wife, Bettina, came from a family of thieves. (This same kind of duality is even at the heart of the opera libretto my brother wrote for me in 1983, which became our work *The Music Teacher.*) Mary was not absent as an influence. My brother's imaginative world often included mental disintegration of one kind or another. My favorite of his early stories, written when he was fourteen or fifteen, was called "Loping Dogs and the Tiles of Time." If I recall rightly, in its central episode a sick doctor meditates on his life while staring at the pattern of interlocking tiles on his bathroom floor (as I did when I had stomachaches).

In many, if not most, of my brother's mature plays, the theme of sickness recurs, with mental, physical, and societal ills seemingly compacted into one. In *The Family Play* there is a retarded or autistic girl; in *Aunt Dan and Lemon* a sickly child who refuses to eat; in *The Fever* and *The Designated Mourner* there are central characters in a state of psychic and physical meltdown in environments that approach the apocalyptic; in *The Hospital Play* everyone is sick, and the hospital appears to be, quite simply, life.

In the family the abstraction of music generally protected me from criticism for lapses of taste or from diverging from the understated reasonableness that characterized much of the work our father seemed to value most. And by the time I myself started going to Putney, at age fifteen, my music was manifestly improving. I had gotten better at extending my ideas, and there were whole movements without problematic passages, or what Mr. Dushkin called "crudities." I seemed to have a natural feeling for melody, harmony, counterpoint, and structure, at least insofar as I used them in my own idiom. Form was something I could almost feel physically, as if it were made of stone rather than notes floating through the air. Starting when I was twelve or thirteen, a musical form would appear in my mind the way a steak appears in a thought bubble over the head of a comic-strip dog: I would feel an appetite to create music that would fill a particular shape. Melodies would come to me easily when I sat down to compose, as if they had been there all along but had been drowned out by the din of life. Both my piano teachers encouraged me to improvise. When I was thirteen, Mrs. Harris, a wonderful teacher who worked with me in the summers, tape-recorded my singing and playing my own operatic version of "Noah's Ark." I wasn't self-conscious, either about my performance or about issues of musical style. "Noah's Ark" was partly improvised, partly composed. It slipped in and out of tonality, exploiting tonal themes for the human and animal characters, and atonal ones for the flood and for God. I see now that even this story could be connected back to Mary since it revolves around animals in pairs that are rescued from oblivion.

During my third summer at Kinhaven I had my first informal composition lessons from a conductor, Eckhart Richter, who had studied composition with Paul Hindemith. He explained some of the elements of the musical language of my new orchestra piece, such as "fourth chords," for which I didn't yet have names; had me make adjustments in some of the rough spots; and suggested some compositional niceties to help unify the piece, such as the use of a muted trumpet playing the theme from the first section of the piece over the passage I had written as the work's ending. These were good lessons that taught me valuable approaches to refining, strengthening, and deepening my work, and gave me a sense of the meaning of the word "craft," of how to consciously improve what had at first come naturally and without effort. To me, composing was a way of speaking, and this piece (it was called *Fantasy for Orchestra*) in particular seemed to speak for me with a kind of urgency. As usual, I came down with some kind of flu before the performance and conducted it as if trying to vanquish a demon. Later the following spring I went to Montpelier, Vermont, to conduct the piece with the Vermont Philharmonic, at which time it felt like a far more normal experience. My brother took the bus from Cambridge, Massachusetts, to play violin in the orchestra, and together we stayed at the home of a local family. Not for the first or for the last time, I noticed that young women encountered in family settings stirred longings in me. I was struck by an instant, if fleeting, crush on the daughter of the house.

When I was seventeen my parents took me on a trip to the Princeton home of the celebrated composer Vincent Persichetti, who taught at Princeton and Juilliard. While my parents stayed downstairs talking with Persichetti's gracious and attractive wife, a concert pianist who was in the process of learning the newest of the many piano sonatas her husband had written for her, Persichetti and I ascended the stairs to his garretlike work studio, where I played him some of my piano pieces. It was one of my first encounters with a truly professional response to my work. I still remember the way he rushed to the piano and dove into his own improvisation based on my ideas. "Why are the accompaniments so stiff?" he asked, pointing to the number of times I had written steady eighth-note chords in my left hand, while the right hand played the melody. "You could do this!" he said, sending volleys of wild figurations hurtling up and down the keyboard—"or this!" His imagination seemed amazingly fertile and accessible to him. He talked about how I could open up the form of the pieces and range more widely, almost into atonal territory, without losing the essential tonal underpinnings of what I had written. As I came back downstairs, feeling almost dizzy with excitement and an expanded sense of music's possibilities, I could see how smitten my father was with Persichetti's wife, and with his artistic lifestyle. My mother smiled beatifically in her bright red lipstick; she was proud of me.

Going to Putney suited my nature and meant that for a few years I was virtually a full-time resident of Vermont, where I was to eventually move twenty years later, and where I still live. Like Kinhaven, Putney encouraged individual expression but, just as importantly, gave students a sense of what people can do together when they collaborate: performing, building things, working in the barn, having discussions, celebrating, traveling for hours singing songs in the back of a truck, hiking through deep woods and falling asleep around a fire far from any town or road. The prevailing view of music was communal too. Many of these school activities affected me positively and negatively at the same time. The sickness that came over me before conducting at Kinhaven was replicated in miniature throughout the week, in chorus, in orchestra, in classes, in group meetings, on buses, in cars. But I also enjoyed myself. It was terribly confusing: I often felt that I was dying when I was most moved or joyful. I was not yet a true "agoraphobic" (only untended children have the freedom to structure their lives around their fears) and had spoken of my anxieties and claustrophobia to no one. In fact I did not know that I was suffering from something that could be articulated at all.

Around the time that Mary was becoming a teenager, the doggedly devoted Miss Anderson, founder of Sandpiper, married an older teacher named Archibald. My parents, who liked people to stay in fixed positions and sometimes seemed to cast acquaintances as beyond human needs, were quite surprised, almost as if Miss Anderson had been the mother superior of a convent who had run off with the gardener. "Archie" loved being around the students at the school and for a few years contributed his welcome male presence to its communal life. But during one of my vacations from Putney, my mother confided in me that she was worried about whether Mrs. Archibald (as she was now known) would choose to continue running Sandpiper or could continue to cope with Mary. Mary was now a sturdy young woman, and she had started to become more tempestuous. At times she would break free from adult control, lashing out when she didn't want to obey an instruction, and even running out onto the beach late at night. I remember my mother suggesting that there could come a point when Mrs. Archibald could no longer "control" Mary. Looking at the blurry photos I have of our family at Sandpiper, I now see to my surprise how slight Mrs. Archibald was.

I learned only recently that Mrs. Archibald had been trying to convince my parents for several years that Mary had outgrown the Sandpiper setting, which had never in fact been intended as a home for mature teenagers. Along with the indications that Mary's condition might be deteriorating, since she was increasingly disruptive and unstable, Mrs. Archibald's own health was declining. In 1964, unbeknownst to me, my parents visited an institution in Delaware—I've called it Briarcliff—which had been recommended to them by, among others, Herta Wertheim. Dr. Wertheim had always hoped that someday Mary might have been able to resume a more normal life. There is tact, regret, and a hint of old Vienna in the letter she wrote to my mother in June 1964, from Ohio:

You have no idea how happy I was with your phone call. This does not happen every day—we are a bit off the path. I was sorry that my optimistic phantasies about Mary were not quite realistic: I had thought of her bicycling to public school, —I guess, Irene's also optimistic reports some years back had been such welcome basis to wish fulfilling dreams. I would love to see a picture of your almost grown daughter.

7

DISLOCATIONS

I n 1966, the year Mary and I turned eighteen, we each crossed an
institutional threshold. In the fall I entered Harvard University.
At the same time, Mrs. Archibald, her health now in decline, was
in the process of closing down Sandpiper. Mary was one of only
three students still on the premises. On September first (our parents' forty-eighth wedding anniversary) Mary was moved to the
home in Delaware where she still lives. This had to be a nerve-
racking moment for my parents. Admission to the new institution,
Briarcliff, could not be assumed, and neither could Mary's even-
tual adjustment to such a new environment. She tended to be ap-
prehensive about the slightest change of routine and disturbed by
the slightest deviation from the expected. Mary had lived in a
home on the ocean with a dozen young people since the age of
eight; it was unclear how she would take to a sprawling campus
housing roughly a thousand people of all ages and types of mental
disabilities in a suburban setting.

In early August, records describing Mary's health, temperament, habits, social problems, and the educational levels she had reached had been forwarded to the school, and she had been tentatively accepted. In a letter addressed to my parents from Briarcliff in mid-August, plans for Mary's visit and a face-to-face interview on August 31 (which happened to be my father's birthday) were laid out. If everything went well, she would be admitted the following day. But there was also a possibility that if she were found to be too acutely disturbed she would have to be sent at least temporarily to a nearby psychiatric hospital to be treated and studied.

Time had run out at Sandpiper. While she knew Mary was very upset by the prospect of leaving the school, Mrs. Archibald had already set its official closing date. It had been three years since she had first told my parents that it was time to move Mary to a new home.

My brother and I accompanied our parents to Briarcliff, where we were met by Mrs. Archibald and Mary. I know now that our parents were even more anxious than usual on the trip down, but I doubt that I was consciously aware of it then. I found out years later that our father had had an upset stomach and needed to spend time in several roadside restrooms on the way. My brother, looking very thin, had just returned from his Fulbright year in India.

On August 31, in addition to interviewing Mary, the doctors at Briarcliff administered the following tests: Wechsler Adult Intelligence Scale; Wide Range Achievement Test; Beery-Buktenica Test of Visual-Motor Integration; Vineland Social Maturity Scale; sentence completion test; projective drawing test. Results showed that she was able to read and write at about the third-grade level and perform the four basic arithmetic operations at a beginning fifth-grade level. They found her particular strengths to be "immediate auditory recall" and "spatial reasoning," while listing her cognitive weaknesses as including "central auditory processing, cause-and-effect understanding, language development, and abstract reasoning."

In the notes I later found in my mother's bureau, I read a description of a similar testing situation. Mary is described as entering the examining room "full of apprehension" and asking numerous questions with which to orient herself, for example, "Who are you?" and frequently, "Are we done now?" "She is a youngster who sees herself as younger than she is," the examiner writes. "She approximates 40% of normal; she has visual-motor problems which leave her at a 4 to 5 year functioning level in visual motor skills. In addition, she has been with younger children and has absorbed this atmosphere and sense of herself." He describes her as being on the verge of screaming at several points during the interview yet, in a "hopeful" sign that she was also capable of controlling and releasing her anxiety, was able to turn these screams into yawns. Summarizing, he writes that, while "not happy with the evaluation," Mary "did her duty."

After Mary was interviewed, the medical staff met with Mrs. Archibald and then with my parents. The team urged my parents to stay for a few days while Mary got settled, but my parents declined this request, as well as an offer of "parental counseling." The interviewers found my parents to be exceptionally anxious people. I can well imagine that there was an atmosphere of mystery surrounding them. My mother was surely holding back the true extent of my father's travel phobias—staying a few days in Delaware would have been sheer torture for him—and guarding her own privacy about why she needed to stay close to him at all times.

Behind all of this was her need to appear as mentally healthy as possible, while maintaining a sense of family specialness. The notes quote her as saying to the interviewers, "We are a very attractive, bright and unusual family." At the end of the interview my parents agreed to sign a release form permitting Briarcliff to send Mary to the psychiatric hospital, should that ever become necessary.

Today I have some of the notes from the day's meetings. Mrs. Archibald told the doctors and staff at Briarcliff that Mary had been retained at Sandpiper under pressure from her parents for three years after it stopped being appropriate. Nevertheless, she had a very close relationship with Mary. She said that Mary needed structure and to have things explained clearly. Her arithmetic was on a third- to fourth-grade level. She particularly liked subtraction but could not tell time. Reading was on a second- to third-grade level. She enjoyed knitting, connect-the-dots books, swimming, playing the piano, and watching television. Mrs. Archibald thought that Briarcliff was a good fit for Mary, even though the unit she would be in, only one out of dozens on the campus, was itself larger than the entire size of Sandpiper. Mary's mother was, however, very agitated about the need for the move.

This had to be a poignant and wrenching moment not only for my parents but for Mrs. Archibald too. When Sandpiper had been converted from a summer camp to a school, Mary and Josie and perhaps one or two others had been the ones to stay on. Mary had lived with Irene (Anderson) Archibald as long as she had lived in New York.

On September 1, the same day that the Sandpiper School in Chatham, Massachusetts, officially closed, Mary was admitted to Briarcliff.

———

Our first visits to Briarcliff after Mary went to live there opened up a world of strangeness I hadn't known existed. The first surprise was the scale of the place. Then there were the residents. We saw lines of obedient adults of all ages, walking in slow, shuffling groups, like tired children at nursery school: tall, skinny people with tiny (microcephalic) heads; heavyset, large-headed adults with drooping eyes and dragging feet; mature men and women with strange gaits, sometimes almost teetering off balance as they walked, like seals perched on their hind flippers, with their hands held up in the air in front of them. Children are often obsessed with normality, trying to determine whether what is true for them is true for others, and reassuring themselves by comparisons with those who don't quite fit on the grid. Here was a whole world of people who apparently did not fit, none of whom could live independently, most of whom were, unlike Mary, visibly marked by their strangeness. If living with Mary had taught me early that the human mold is a rough generalization, full of variables, potential flaws, and botched patches—a lesson everyone has to learn eventually—the sight of the residents at Briarcliff greatly expanded upon this message. Just being at Briarcliff induced a kind of vertigo in an impressionable young person, calling into question the order of things and demonstrating that nothing could be taken for granted. For at least a time, children can generally believe in a fixity of categories—that old is old, young is young, beauty is permanent, a mind is a mind. I had an early lesson in human frailty. As Mary's twin, ignorant as I was about the cause of her impairments and with our twinship an almost taboo subject, I often found myself wondering if it was only a matter of time before the magic glue that held my own brain together would lose its adhesive properties and I would join the lines of shuffling institutional dependents at Briarcliff.

Whatever anxieties Mary had suffered in adjusting to Briarcliff were not apparent when we saw her there, nor did she show the slightest surprise about her new companions. Briarcliff seemed, in most ways, a fortunate choice. The campus was divided into small units linked by pleasant tree-lined paths. In one respect Mary's experience on the Cape was nearly replicated: her individual unit, a likable one-story house with a gazebo and picnic table outside, was home to roughly a dozen housemates, overseen by a live-in administrator and rotating shifts of aides. The residents of the home were all women, and they ranged in age from eighteen to eighty. The campus was dotted with such homes, some housing women, some men. There was also a section of the campus used as a day school for school-age children with learning disorders. For a few years, Mary continued to attend some classes there, but her days as a student were ending. The older men and women came together for work—wrapping packages, putting together boxes of goods, assembly-line style—and, on special occasions, for parties and dances.

Mary was now a working young adult. She drew a small salary for her package-wrapping, which was put in an account for her, and from which she could make purchases. (One year she bought herself a television set.)

Although she no longer took piano lessons, she continued to play the pieces she had learned at Sandpiper, and even one she remembered from musicals heard on recordings at home in New York, on a small upright piano in her unit. At church, which she attended regularly, she played hymns, or Irving Berlin's "Always," or "The Hills Are Alive" from *The Sound of Music*. With repetition she had foreshortened some of these songs and played others with an oddly unmetered rhythm. She would sit down at the piano and begin playing almost in one motion, looking at the keyboard with intent seriousness, her plump, fleshy, small hands becoming her entire focus. Playing the piano she looked exactly the way our father did editing manuscripts. Some years earlier she had been taught accompanying left-hand chords that, while they minimized hand motions, also made for momentary dissonances, making one wonder what modern music would sound like to her.

During our visits she could become temperamental about playing for us. Somehow, perhaps because we were so used to the calming, happiness-inducing effect of our father's piano playing, a visit would never feel complete if she didn't play. She clearly felt this pressure, but there was also an unfamiliar edginess to her pianistic ambivalence, as if our request stirred some new resistance that hadn't been there at Sandpiper. At the very least, like me, she evidently preferred to play for strangers than for her family. If, despite this, she agreed to play, we would all be pleased. Then my father might play a song as well, and I might accompany Mary in "Heart and Soul" or another piece we both knew. During these jam sessions the other residents would take obvious pleasure, and Mary would sometimes not be able to repress a grin and a special laugh, which would make her eyes squint with amusement.

There were many new elements in Mary's life at Briarcliff. One was medication. So far in her life, her mind had been left to its own devices. Her inner chemistry had not been interfered with, apart from routine medicines taken for childhood ailments and illnesses. Now she seemed to exhibit some new tendencies as a result of whatever she was taking. (Years later I learned that one medication she took at the time was the antipsychotic Thorazine.) She seemed reasonably contented but also quieter. Sometimes she had a subdued, submissive, heavy-lidded look, from which she would glance up almost furtively. Her hands had developed a slight tremor, and her fingers seemed permanently curved inward. Her walking seemed jerkier. The sharp attack and mechanical inflection of her speech seemed accentuated. Along with simply aging, she was showing new physical signs of her differentness. Was it the medication? Or simply that I was noticing these signs more because of seeing her so infrequently?

Briarcliff was founded in 1913 by an idealistic woman with a particular interest in teaching mentally retarded children. Intended as a humane alternative to the stark conditions of hospitals for the emotionally disturbed and the mentally ill, it aimed to do systematically and with patience what few families could: teach some social and personal skills to those who could never function independently in the adult world. Its philosophy was to patiently train those whose mental disabilities and low IQs put them outside normal society to at least function more successfully in social situations, and to help them learn to behave in a docile manner in public settings—at restaurants, in shopping expeditions, or at the movies— and to deal with simple tasks in the public realm. In the early days of the institution there were even dress balls where the men and women were brought together, the men in suits, the women in gowns and wearing white gloves, and taught how to bow and to waltz. With little or no insight into what their buried inner gifts might potentially make possible for them, the goal was at least to help them broaden out and participate in some "normal" activities. This was an upscale place; the mission was gentle and, for its day, progressive, a far cry from the world of squalor, abuse, and horror that sometimes awaited those placed in public institutions.

Between the ages of eighteen and twenty-five, Mary did grow increasingly able to take care of herself and to express her needs—to dress and make herself presentable, to wait her turn, to ask for things politely. As always, routines suited her: she learned to smile and say "cheese" when posing for a photo; to carefully stack plates in the dining hall; to faithfully do her chores at the vocational center. At the same time, no doubt for a variety of reasons, she could no longer "pass for normal." She lost the delicacy and serenity of look she had once had, and her physical motions became more jerky and oddly articulated. Yet, in a sense—despite our mother's wish to exemplify mental health and family togetherness (there were occasions when, bizarrely, she compared us to, of all people, the Kennedy family)—no one in our family could have ever passed for "normal." Strangely, wonderfully, as she aged, Mary resembled my brother and father all the more. She exuded a kind of focused seriousness and carried herself with something of their gravitas, dignity, and authority.

As always, the various timbres of her speaking voice remained terraced, like the dynamics in baroque music, with little modulation or rise and fall from one level to another. She can murmur a whole thought to herself as if in one word ("maryshawnwillhave-milkandcookies"); she can enunciate every syllable with a broad smile, teeth bared, as if at an elocution class ("Milk and COOKies"); she can send the words out with the sound of a plaintive keening if she is worried ("Mary Shawn is not going out today"), in each instance sounding like a different person. What is rare is a sense of true verbal exchange. Emotion comes through her eyes and facial expressions, but rarely through her choice of words. Mary has an entire language at her disposal, but words are only a small part of it.

Sandpiper had had an almost magical, fairy-tale air about it, and furthermore was pointedly a school, a place where an atmosphere of hope was implicit in the instructional routine and evident in the progress the children made there. It seemed a place where unusual people were embraced. Briarcliff had been founded in a similar spirit but was ultimately more frankly custodial. It was probably as comfortable a setting for mentally disabled adults as existed in the country at the time, yet there was no denying that it was an institution. The hopes for Mary had shrunk from those connected to her own optimal achievements to those that made for an orderly, manageable life. Since her weight was considered a problem, control of her diet was a priority. She was to continue to learn to take care of herself properly as independently as possible—brushing her teeth, bathing, getting dressed; to master learning how to behave in groups going out to a restaurant or to the movies or, in the summer, to the beach. In short, the socialization begun at Sandpiper, where she learned how to say "Yes, please" when offered a second helping of ice cream, and not just "Yes!" was continued, but not the development of her intellectual skills—her reading, her handwriting, her arithmetic, her drawing, her piano playing—which might benefit no one other than herself, but whose limits had not necessarily been reached.

My parents still received letters and cards from Mary, as they had when she lived at Sandpiper, but these were often written in a mature script that was not Mary's own and, however accurate, didn't reflect her grammar and syntax, used words she wouldn't use, and didn't convey her personality. In short, they were ghost-written. By contrast, my father's notes to our mother used expressions that only Mary herself would have used. For example, he could write "I love you, Mommy," because Mary had learned to say or echo the phrase "I love you," even though otherwise she rarely used the first-person pronoun in a sentence. One card from Briarcliff read:

Dear Mom and Dad,

Thank you for the nice Christmas gifts. I had a very nice holiday. I visited with some people and Miss Sharon took me to her house for Christmas, and I opened some gifts there. Here is a picture of me dressed up for Halloween. I went as Santa Clause. The costume you sent was beautiful. I got to wear that when we went trick or treating. Did you like the Christmas picture of me? Take care.

At the bottom of the letter Mary's name would be written in capital letters—no longer in the cursive hand she had dutifully practiced at Sandpiper—with the "Y" pointing in to the right, looking like a "t." Perhaps this was her actual handwriting. Otherwise, even putting aside the fact that we were Jewish, nothing in such letters seemed to specifically evoke Mary, even while they conveyed accurate information about her life and showed how much care and attention she was receiving. She had never called her parents "Mom and Dad," and she certainly wouldn't have ever said "Take care." She would have called the costume they had sent "beautiful" only in answer to the question, "Isn't the costume beautiful?" and then would have most likely responded with the one-word assertion, "Isn'thecostumebeautiful." And beyond the correct usage of tenses and pronouns, what most jarred with the reality of Mary's character was the letter's confident grasp of the distinction between "you" and "me"—"your" perceptions, your world, and "my" world, the ability to picture someone else's view of herself. ("Here is a picture . . ." "Did you like the Christmas picture of me?") And, given her obsession with holidays, she would also surely have spelled "Santa Claus" correctly.

Mary did indeed continue to mature and develop as she aged, but only within the confines set for her at Briarcliff. Along with the guilt my brother and I have carried with us about her overall fate was additional guilt about the mystery of her untapped potential. What if she had somehow been able to stay forever at Sandpiper? Might she have continued to make the kind of progress she had originally made in her years there? Might she have continued to stay, or at least to seem, more serene and youthful? Or was her trajectory preset, with the years eight to eighteen predestined to be the ones where significant intellectual growth could occur?

As a child, it had sometimes seemed to me that Mary contained great wisdom that because of some unwritten law she could not divulge. It was comforting to think that she belonged to a purposefully contemplative world, that she was like a monk on a mountaintop in Tibet, or an Indian seer who had taken a vow of silence, living on the streets of Calcutta, observing rituals on behalf of mankind in general. At Harvard, when I thought of Mary, it was as if she had become a mythological figure.

I had been discouraged so often from seeking to know more about her life that I rarely remembered that I wanted to. Sometimes I tried to imagine her experience: having pains or torments for which I had no language and for which, even if I could speak properly, there *is* no common language; or tried to picture how she viewed her parents, or her brothers, or her own changing body as she aged. I was dimly aware that while she did not understand "my" types of categories, the reverse was also true. She had rules and categories, and no doubt emotions, that I was not privy to.

When I thought of her, I might just as well have been wondering what a bird feels when it sings or when it flies from place to place and makes a decision to land here and not there. How and where does it register its experience of not singing, and then singing; of flying, and then alighting? What are its physical sensations; what are its "thoughts"? How can one enter into the bird's mind, or imagine its sensations, or what it is like to pay attention to what a bird pays particular attention to, and to ignore what it ignores? But mostly I found it mentally exhausting to continually wonder about Mary, who was, after all, not a bird, but fully human. Mostly, I tried not to think of her.

There is a saying, "Youth is wasted on the young," which certainly has a ring of truth to it. Yet one would also be justified in saying that only young people are strong enough to survive youth. When I think of the uncertainties and shocks I kept bumping up against in my childhood, which was by any measure a very fortunate one, I wince even now. And when I think of how baffling life must have been for Mary as a child, and of the many layers of terror she must have experienced when she passed from one stage of growing up to another, I am stunned trying to imagine how she tolerated it.

Among the hardships of even a normal youth is never knowing whether what is happening to you, inside or outside, will be a permanent or just a transient experience. If you are jilted by a girl, or you fail an exam, or have become a nervous wreck, or you are sick, you do not yet know if you are doomed to a life of solitude, intellectual failure, chronic anxiety, or illness. Have you finally been revealed to be an idiot? Will girls ever like you? Are you dying? Are you a nervous wreck, or only in certain circumstances?

Whereas at Putney, the cloistered farm school, I had been sociable and relatively confident, in the competitive, impersonal, cosmopolitan atmosphere of Harvard I drew into myself, spending an inordinate time alone in my room fantasizing about women and music and contemplating life's issues. It would never have occurred to me to use a word like "depressed" to describe my inwardness, and not once did I connect my feelings of solitude with being a twin, or with "unresolved feelings" from childhood. I noticed only that my anxieties about sitting in groups and riding in elevators had increased. I also felt increasingly religious. Although I no longer attended Catholic Mass, I was particularly fond of medieval and Renaissance art and kept a print of a Fra Angelico *Annunciation* and a crucifixion scene on my wall, alongside a street scene by Van Gogh and a sentimental portrait of a voluptuous peasant woman with her blouse falling off by the French painter Jean-Baptiste Greuze. (At Oxford, my brother hung the very same *Annunciation* on his wall. Neither of us consciously associated Fra Angelico's "Mary" with our sister.)

In the winter of my freshman year my beloved piano teacher Miss Dillon died. She had spent the year in Vienna, sending me postcards from the homes of Beethoven, Mozart, and Schubert, and had written me a long letter in which she told me to "always write from the heart." Her husband, Charles, wrote to me that her own heart had been ailing for some months and that she had died on New Year's Eve after raising a glass of champagne to toast him and their son.

During my first two college years the quality of my classwork was wildly uneven. I did well in Renaissance Painting and in Japanese Art. I received an A in Philosophy on the strength of a paper about death, in which I argued that we cannot help but imagine death in terms of things we know. I then explored the many ways in which we betray the fact that we have illusions about something that is in fact pure nothingness. By contrast, I barely passed German. Transfixed by the stunning beauty of the young instructor, with whom I had once had a brief exchange on the subject of Alban Berg's steamy opera *Lulu*, I managed to oversleep the final exam. If this derived from my unconscious wish to speak with her one more time in person, that wish was granted. I pleaded my case with her, but only received a grade of D plus. However, I still retain a vivid memory of her face and voice, and of the way her legs looked in fishnet stockings.

Most humiliatingly, I failed a course in Indian History for which I had actually worked quite hard. Some of the course readings on Buddhism and Hinduism had fascinated me and inspired me to write a paper on Gandhi's religious attitudes. However, this was at the expense of the historical and economic aspects of the course, and even of readings on some historical figures of religious significance. A dense biography of King Ashoka (third century BC) remained opened at page six on my desk all term, with its lizard green cover, onionskin pages, and tiny dark print becoming a kind of permanent shrine to my boredom. My tendency to panic flourished in exams, when my resistance to being hemmed in combined combustibly with the all-too-real stresses and time constraints of having my competence tested. In Biology my interest was sufficient to carry me through this three-hour ordeal and I did adequately. But in Indian History I was prepared to write only about Gandhi and religion. My crudely sketched map of India was a sorry inverted triangle with token marks where I hoped Bombay, Calcutta, and the Ganges might be located. My "imaginary dialogue" between Maynard Keynes, Nehru, and Muhammad Ali Jinnah on the subject of partition trailed off into silence after a series of niceties ("Hello, Maynard." "How are you, Jawaharlal?"). I failed the exam, and later my paper on Gandhi was returned to me unread.

I did learn, but in unexpected places: when I looked into a drop of water under a microscope in biology class and found there just as much feverish activity as could be seen by the naked eye in an anthill; when I dissected a live rat and saw with my own eyes the tangled arteries, beating heart, and tiny rubberlike organs that animated him; when I looked through the lens of the gigantic telescope in the Harvard Observatory past a network of distant stars, at the rings of Saturn and the pitted orange surface of Mars. I did not ever consciously relate all these small epiphanies back to Mary, or to the mystery of her humanity. I only knew that I was somehow hungry for understanding and looking for a meaning in things.

Socially I felt disengaged from my peers. I had a circle of taciturn and scientifically minded dinner companions who couldn't have been more different from my wild and theatrical friends from high school. In their midst I became the flamboyant one, but somehow my heart wasn't in it, or, truthfully, in them. I relished time spent with my older companions, close friends of my brother's, five years older than me, with whom I went to movies, watched the news, cooked spaghetti, smoked cigars, had sparkling conversations, and felt comfortable and free. I had a wonderful roommate, Steve, who played the violin in the Harvard-Radcliffe Orchestra and shared my passion for music. I also became close to two graduate students, a glamorous female literature student and a brilliant male writer who was as fanatically obsessed with Nabokov as I was with Stravinsky. In their heady company I sometimes had intimations of possessing an intellect myself, and of horizons beyond my musical ones.

In these years—the late sixties—one could not be a college student without encountering drugs, any more than one could avoid hearing the Beatles or being, at the very least, preoccupied by the escalating Vietnam War. Despite my esoteric musical tastes, I still loved some of the rock music of the time, and in spite of my claustrophobia in crowds, I participated in demonstrations and sit-ins against the war. But nothing could have attracted me less than the notion of the "consciousness expansion" promised by drugs, since I already felt I was just barely husbanding the stability of my mind. My mental equilibrium was already frequently shaken by anxieties and unexpected bouts of queasy listlessness, and there were moments when I feared I was becoming unhinged. Leaving parties where the rooms had been so dark and wreathed in marijuana smoke one couldn't even tell who was there—and no one seemed to care anyway—I would become preoccupied that even though I hadn't smoked it myself, pot's magical elixir had entered me and that, in my case, once inside, would never leave me. I would feel light-headed walking home, would imagine that the streetlights were shining luridly and the buildings were swaying, and worry that my "consciousness" had "expanded" permanently beyond reality and would remain that way forever.

On weekends I worked as a volunteer teacher of "music appreciation" at Bridgewater State Prison, where the famous "Boston Strangler" was currently incarcerated. I would bring recordings of Bach, or Tchaikovsky, or even modern music, from the Harvard music library, and at the prison would be handed a beige-colored carrier that looked like a child's suitcase containing a cheap phonograph not unlike the one Mary had played opera arias on in our New York apartment a dozen years before. To get to the "classroom" I would pass (voluntarily!) through a succession of locked metal doors that would open and then close behind me to the sounds of buzzers, and walk escorted through a labyrinth of identical-looking shiny green corridors to a small cell-like room. The men and I would sit around a table listening to the music on the tiny phonograph, and I would say a little bit about the lives of the composers and maybe add a word or two of a technical nature about what we were hearing. Mostly this was about giving these men, some of whom were guilty of terrible acts and were expected to remain in prison forever, a break from grim routine. The men were not only criminals, they were clearly mentally ill and seemed to me to be, like Mary, heavily medicated. Every so often they talked about themselves and spoke dispassionately and blandly, almost wistfully, of impulses, sexual or violent, over which they had previously had no control. But sometimes they would actually listen to the music coming from the little machine, and sometimes in the windowless chamber an imaginary window would briefly open onto impassioned communal singing, or soaring balletic melodies, full of ecstatic longing. Leaving through the labyrinth I would feel my muscles loosen bit by bit as the buzzers sounded and I was finally released into the night air, crossing the last enclosure, a courtyard encased in cement walls and lit by blinding klieg lights. I was always conscious at that moment that I was *outside*, a miraculously free person, and that there were those who were inside.

In these and in other ways I unknowingly carried Mary around with me.

Meanwhile my own music had become the perfect illustration of the state of my psyche: it was fragmented and disconnected. During my first year at Harvard I had finally been thrust into an environment in which my being a young composer wasn't so special. Even one of my own new friends had had a piece played by a major orchestra when he was a child. I needed to fulfill various requirements in the music program to even be considered for admission into a composition seminar, and completing them would take two years. When in spite of not being an official composition student I had a new piece played at a student concert, it was, I noticed, the most old-fashioned-sounding contribution on the program, and its language seemed suddenly naïve, even to me. It was the first time I heard one of my pieces in a truly public context. I knew that I needed formal composition lessons, and in my second year I started going by bus every week to Lexington, Massachusetts, to study with a teacher from the New England Conservatory, Francis Judd Cooke. Rather than interfere directly in my composing, Cooke's approach was to introduce me to as much great music as possible. We studied the harmonies in Stravinsky's *Oedipus Rex* and *The Rake's Progress*—trying to tease out how their individual and contemporary tonality was achieved using such familiar materials. Why, Cooke asked, did the "simple" D major and minor triads played when Oedipus finally realized his own guilt sound so shatteringly memorable—as if the whole score, like the narrative, had converged on that moment? Together we studied Bartók's *Bluebeard's Castle*, Schoenberg's *Moses und Aron*, Berg's *Wozzeck*. At Harvard I discovered the libraries. I realized that I was a "completist." In Lamont Library I found every uncollected Salinger story ever printed in a magazine, even the early *New Yorker* story featuring Holden Caulfield before *The Catcher in the Rye* had been conceived. In Hilles, I listened to every note written by Stravinsky. In the Paine Hall music library, on the heels of hearing the mind-boggling *Concord Sonata* for the first time, I explored all the songs and chamber and orchestral music of Charles Ives. During this time I had three little musical epiphanies, and they all had to do with Mozart. The first occurred when I was in a restaurant and could not concentrate on the conversation because the music playing in the background was so compelling. The music turned out to be Mozart's Clarinet Quintet, and it made me realize that whenever Mozart was playing I had an indefinable feeling that made time seem to stop. I realized from this something that I still can only struggle to put into words: that in some magical way the notes and rhythms of music could convey an essence about existing and time passing, could make a moment in time audible. The next little epiphany occurred when I was attending Mozart's *Die Entführung aus dem Serail*, an early opera of his with a remarkably silly plot. At the end of the evening I realized that the overall design of the work had etched itself in my mind as it progressed, that the breaks between recitatives and arias and even between acts were merely spaces between points in a huge canvas, and that the key relationships from one section to the next were like small chord progressions writ large. The entire evening was one piece of music. The third moment, almost the reverse of this one, occurred when I was on a train returning to Harvard from New York studying the score to a Mozart piano sonata. I realized looking at the piece note by note, as the train jostled the music in my lap, that the language generated by the progression from one interval to the next represented the compression of thought to an astounding density; that only by looking at music very, very slowly—much more slowly than it is ever played—can one begin to understand the universe it contains. These experiences, and others like them, gradually eradicated the sense I had had when I was a child that music had become more complex in recent periods and that earlier music was less relevant to the world of the present or to what I might hope to compose myself.

With the start of my official music classes, however, my own music entered a personal "dark ages." Gone was my spontaneous joy in composing, my identification with the notes I was putting down, that flow of ideas that, however flawed or immature, still conveyed a sense of direction and purpose. Instead of losing myself, and thereby finding myself, in the process of making up music, I had become increasingly and painfully self-aware, checking my every move against the judgment of imagined arbiters. I no longer trusted myself. What seemed to matter most was not the natural progression of my own musical thoughts but the "rightness" of each individual moment, checked against some internal almanac of "acceptable" moments. Even if nonetheless some details of my new pieces still managed to be musically appealing, the pieces as a whole were nothing more than useless assemblages, patchwork quilts of moments pointing to references outside the compositions themselves. Had I been in a position to take these pieces to a seer (preferably a Buddhist one), perhaps the seer might have told me, "My son, if you have lost your music, it is because you have placed too great a burden on it."

I nevertheless benefited enormously from studies with two Harvard teachers. One was the tormented, brilliant, intuitively rhapsodic composer Leon Kirchner. Kirchner had been a student of the great Arnold Schoenberg (about whom, thirty years after college, I wrote a book). I can't say that I learned from Kirchner the composition teacher as much as I learned from hearing his music in his presence, watching him conduct, and, particularly, hearing him play the piano. Like Schoenberg, Kirchner never forgot that he was part of a long and inexhaustibly rich tradition. Despite his large ego and equally large personality, he was deeply humble in the face of the works of Mozart, Bach, or Brahms he conducted and played. Like my teacher Miss Dillon, Kirchner produced a beautifully weighty, rounded tone on the piano when he was illustrating his ideas for us at the instrument, speaking in his distinctively mellow, almost leathery, Brooklyn-accented voice. In particular, I remember the sound he produced playing the descending thirds in the first Intermezzo of Brahms's op. 119 piano pieces. Although I was among the youngest and, at that time, least confident of his students, he treated me and my compositions kindly. Fortunately, over the years since then I was able to convey to him how much his teaching had meant to me. His influence went beyond music to include an attitude about life. Rather than court a small audience of new music enthusiasts or, on the other hand, adapt his standards to fit the expectations of conservative traditional audiences, he pursued his own fiercely independent visions of beauty. The coloristic originality and substantiveness of these visions was of a subtle kind that did not give off an aura of innovation. His music was almost too poetic and elegant for the time in which it was written. It was also emotionally explosive and ecstatic; it did not have the cool temperature characteristic of much of the better postwar music. Despite his renown among musicians, Kirchner, like Schoenberg, did not really receive what one might consider his "due" in terms of public acclaim. But from an artistic standpoint, he led a fulfilling life. He was a musical giant, plugged into music's depths.

The other teacher who left an indelible imprint on me was the pianist Luise Vosgerchian. Temperamentally, Luise was Kirchner's exact opposite: animated and sparkling and sharply precise, where he was turbulent and searching. During my most dispirited period at Harvard, when I was studying baroque figured bass in her class and occasionally having one of my pieces performed, she took me aside and said, "I believe in you." I never forgot it. It was also Luise who wrote a letter to her former teacher Nadia Boulanger in Paris, recommending that I be accepted as her student there following my graduation.

Once Mary had moved to Briarcliff, our periodic family trips across the George Washington Bridge and south to Delaware continued for several years. Excursions to see Mary no longer had a romantic, nostalgic feeling to them. Since we could accomplish the round trip in a day, there were no glittering stays at plush hotels or nights of music to cushion the intrinsic poignancy of the visits. In Mary's first years at Briarcliff my brother was away at Oxford studying politics, philosophy, and economics, and I made some of the trips with my parents alone. On a few occasions I brought a friend with me. On the way, my father would, as always, work on manuscripts in the comfortable limousine backseat. But the route across the tall and often crowded bridge and down the unvaryingly straight and bleakly industrial Route 1 in New Jersey cast a gloomy pall over him. There were times when he reached for a little pill in a small round container he carried in his suit pocket. My own burgeoning anxieties made me dread the ride too. If there was still relief and emotion on the return trip, still the sense that once again the original family unit had been reconstituted and that we had reconnected with the mystery that was Mary, the sense of catharsis was mitigated by sorrow that the hopes raised at Sandpiper were in the past. While my brother and I were forging ahead in our lives, Mary was remaining, in some respects, a child. In the car our mother would say how much better Mary seemed this time, and unless I was in a quarrelsome mood, we would all agree with her.

8

BINARY STARS

Everything conspired to make me feel remote from Mary as the two of us grew older: the distance required to reach her new home, greatly inflated by the dread my parents, and later I myself, felt about traveling generally; the ring of secrets and taboos that created hidden land mines in our family's conversational terrain, and had somehow expanded to encompass most of the difficult aspects of our lives; even the letters and cards from Briarcliff that tried to bridge the gap between her world and ours by erasing her eccentricities and substituting in their place a kind of generic "normalcy." Over the years Mary had almost seemed to become a fiction, as if her actual life was too painful to contemplate. And underneath all of this there was the built-in distance between her reality and ours, the unfathomable inaccessibility of her way of experiencing things.

Looking back on the young man I was in 1970, leaving for Europe to study music with Boulanger, somehow hoping to be a composer, at the same time having very little concept of what that would mean from a practical point of view, I see someone who was lonely without realizing it. I was lonely not simply as we all are, but as someone is who is distant from what is real. I had internalized my parents' efforts to circumscribe my understanding of their lives and my own, and had gradually started to become even estranged from the creative impulse inside me that had first come to my rescue when I was ten years old. Part of this was just the self-consciousness and fear common in most young adults finding their way. The other part represented a kind of distance from reality and self. I had almost succeeded in forgetting that I was a twin, but at an enormous cost.

There was a place inside me that was still nestled up to Mary, comfortably entwined with her. But this place in me, this buried essence from our infancy, had become an embarrassment, an embarrassment I felt even in my own heart. This place, this memory of being, in a sense, a part of Mary, didn't fit with the life I was living or with the effort I was making to use my mind in ways she couldn't, or with the future I was supposedly moving toward.

And on the surface I did continue moving forward. At first I felt little fear leaving for Europe on my own to study music, or about separating from my parents. True, the separation was only partial. They were still paying my way (as they did for the next two years) and made nothing of the cost of my living for two years in Paris, let alone of the expensive Atlantic crossing by ocean liner I had asked for. (Although willing to fly, I already preferred not to.)

It is presumably a rare person who, at the age of twenty-one, doesn't feel some dread about all that cannot yet be known, about how their lives will turn out, about what fortunes and misfortunes will befall them and when. But precisely because it is unknowable, the future for young people who are not in dire circumstances still seems to hold infinite possibilities for joy and is limited only by the limits of their imaginations. Their dread is mitigated by a gigantic physical appetite for life, as if the future were a perfect juicy orange cut in half on a summer table, or the gently smiling naked Venus of Urbino in Titian's painting, waiting, ready to be embraced, to be enfolded, to be loved. This appetite for life overwhelmed my senses as I traveled across the ocean, surrounded by water and sky, as if freed from everything that had happened to me so far. Looking out at sunset from the ship's deck at the vastness of the ocean, I felt a sense of joyful excitement and creative anticipation. The awe-inspiring expanse of water seemed emblematic of immensities of freedom and possibility, not of emptiness and solitude.

I did not recognize that for me separation and apartness had a very individual meaning. All the issues having to do with my parents and my brother that had never been discussed in my childhood paled by comparison to the unresolved dissonances of my original relationship with Mary ("original" as in "origin"), my love for her, and the abruptness with which our lives had diverged.

In Mary's and my case, twinship was a story of profound togetherness followed by ever-widening degrees of separation. Every effort had been made to distract and distance me from my true relatedness to Mary, from any possible meaning inherent in the fact that we had gestated together, been born on the same day, been greeted with amazement as twins, spent our early months lying next to each other in the same crib, and had grown up in our first years, different as our experiences were, alongside each other, always the same age, moving forward on parallel paths. From the moment my parents realized that there was something wrong with

Mary, we were separated. First she was down the hall from me, keeping my brother up at night with her screams. As she increasingly became the center of family concerns—a source of worry and anxiety and exhaustion—our original togetherness became increasingly painful to mention. Then she was simply absent, reduced to a kind of shimmering nostalgic image, an essentially static, mythical being: always "improving," yet always staying the same and never actually getting anywhere, like poor Sawdust running forever on the little wheel in his cage.

But before we were separated I had always felt I understood Mary. Her unpredictable moods were deeply familiar—beyond familiar, they constituted my world at least as much as my mother's comforting embrace—and like any twins, we had developed a way of communicating in a language of gestures, looks, and vocal inflections.

Later we became like binary stars, the kind that can sometimes only be detected by astronomers because of evidence that one star is subject to the unseen effects of another, as when there is an otherwise inexplicable Doppler effect discerned in its emitted light. I became like a binary star pretending not to be one. Mary and I were orbiting individually, but subject to each other's gravitational pull. That Mary was even less knowable than the average human being didn't change the fact that she and I were linked, and even in many ways alike. I too had a strong autistic dimension in my solitary childhood pursuits: performances for unseen audiences, secret participation in religious ceremonies foreign to those of my ancestors, and later on an obsessive focus on the writing of music, much of which was heard only in my head. And music is in any case the most intangible of the art forms, and the one most subject to inscrutable hidden laws. I was in fact instinctively trying very hard to keep the early communication Mary and I had between us alive within me, and the public aspect of music was only a secondary matter, one fraught with the anxiety that this hidden inner world might be invaded or taken away from me; hence my torments about my work being performed. Mary's indecipherable rituals could also be seen as parallel to those of my parents and brother, in all three of whom strange private agendas often determined outwardly sensible routines. There is no sharp drop-off point between what we deem normal in people and what we do not; the differences can be put on a sloping grade, even if at certain points the slope becomes steep.

The loss of Mary as an acknowledged presence in my daily world had been transformed into a kind of mythologizing, my grief at her sudden, virtually noiseless forced departure from the family into a terror about our separation that I didn't even know I carried within me. This terror was not about growing up, but about being finally free enough from the family ethos to feel the anguish and trauma of loss I had already experienced at the age of eight. Perhaps for Mary herself that separation had been a positive thing. It had indeed appeared to be. For me the disaster needed to have been acknowledged. "Growing up" therefore had a special meaning for me: to grow up and flourish would mean leaving Mary irrevocably behind without having ever reconnected with her or properly experienced the emotions stirred by no longer having her near me; to leave her behind without finding a way of taking her with me.

Instead of comfortably proceeding through the next stage of my life, I did so while experiencing ever-escalating spirals of panic. The panic had been building up for a long time.

In Paris I spent two years studying with Nadia Boulanger, one of the most remarkable figures in twentieth-century music. Boulanger had a near-encyclopedic knowledge of music, a phenomenal ear, a peerless ability to instruct students in the fundamentals of music in a holistic fashion that only increased their love of the materials. She was a colossally realized human being, still radiating intelligence and energy at age eighty-three, continuing to teach her ten-hour-a-day schedule and to conduct. As commanding and formidable as she was, she was also disarmingly personal. Although some of her students trembled in her presence, I did not. I had always felt uneasy in the presence of those who wanted me to be polite or to behave myself or to be falsely cheerful or to avoid discussing distressing things, but Boulanger only wanted to talk about art and about what mattered most in life. For me, her own fearlessness was somehow contagious, and in her presence I felt at the protected heart of things. Perhaps I also related to her life story, which was indelibly affected by the untimely death of her sister Lili, who was already a major composer, at the age of twenty-four.

I also knew that Boulanger's judgments originated from such a high plane of reference that they might not always apply to me. When I first arrived in Paris my music, then vaguely "Stravinskian," was not particularly coherent, more like a tag sale of musical scraps imitating my favorite living composer than like good compositions. To help me get back to a more organic way of working, along with studying with Boulanger I sought the instruction and guidance of a composer who had himself studied with "Mademoiselle" many years before. Pierre Petit was now the director of the École Normale de Musique, and when I first met him it was in fact in the Salle Stravinsky of the conservatory. When I played through my most recent orchestral score for him, he shook his head and pointed to the portrait of Stravinsky on the wall. "We all love Stravinsky. And we salute him," he said, bowing to the portrait. "But we don't need to write like him." Petit much preferred my earlier piano pieces, which were tinged with jazz harmonies and suggestions of midcentury American lyricism, and which also conveyed a natural musical train of thought and had their own sense of form. Over the next months Petit helped me start to get back to writing in my own way. Boulanger never knew that I studied with Petit on the side, and the best piece I wrote under Petit's guidance, a rather somber theme and variations, struck her as false to my nature. When I played it for her, she described it as sounding "like Schoenberg." "You are more direct than that," she told me. I knew that the piece had come very naturally to me, and that its angular contours and dark mood held together much better than my Stravinskian scraps. Despite her reservations, she took the care to compliment a series of descending tenths in the left hand near the end of the theme, and she also programmed the piece on one of her evening concerts. I was beyond grateful to both Pierre Petit and Boulanger, and the thought that Boulanger had enough confidence in me to tell me that in her opinion I was a composer helped sustain me during the many times over the ensuing years when I doubted myself.

In my first year in Paris I was lucky in love. I was involved in a serene, sensuous romance with a delightful eighteen-year-old French girl, then studying anthropology, who happened to be the daughter of old friends of my parents. The relationship eventually lasted for seven years. I had always found it easier to make friends with women than with men. But when it came to love itself, I seemed especially drawn to women who, like Mary, were in some ways out of reach and mysterious. I needed women with whom I could establish an intimate private rapport not entirely comprehensible to my parents, but I also needed some illusion of a quasi-familial tie. Besides being beautiful, lively, and smart, my French girlfriend had the triple advantage of being "other" (from another culture, and with English as a second language), at times emotionally elusive and diffident (fostering the privacy of our rapport), and yet still connected to the world of my childhood.

My second year in Paris, the year that I moved into an apartment with her, was also the year in which my father suffered a heart attack during the Christmas holidays. Although I wanted to return to New York in December to see him, my mother told me that it might scare him if I did so, and that I should wait until the summer. The logic and wisdom behind her caution escaped me, simply confirming once again that our family had managed to make a near religion of denial. As my brother points out today, our mother's belief almost seemed to be that it is not a heart attack that kills you, but rather *acknowledging* that you have had a heart attack.

It was the first time that I ever felt deeply uneasy about being far from home. Suddenly the awesome vastness of the Atlantic Ocean, over which I had traveled to France in a mood of exhilaration, seemed like an obstacle that would prevent me from ever seeing my parents again. Although I was now twenty-two years old, a childlike terror swept through me. I felt like a six-year-old who has confidently climbed up a tree and suddenly realizes that he cannot climb down. Whatever it was that had made me sick when my music was being performed, or against which I seemed to be fighting when I was conducting at music camp, now started to take a more encompassing form. It felt as if I were walking with leaden steps, facing into a heavy wind wherever I tried to move.

This agoraphobia, which has hampered me since, created a strange state of mind combining sorrow, guilt, and existential dread, and invaded my body with a tremulous dis-ease.

When I actually returned from France with my girlfriend in the summer of 1972, I felt like a more vulnerable person than I had been when I left for France. But since I also found myself on my own financially, I was luckily saved from getting bogged down in my problems by needing to find work. My girlfriend and I moved into a two-room apartment in a small brownstone on the Upper West Side, and she began attending graduate school. I began teaching music at a small private high school and in the preparatory division of a conservatory, and I applied to Juilliard for graduate work in composition. Teaching helped me focus on the needs and personalities of others. At night and in between times, I worked on my compositions on the same upright piano that my parents had had the foresight and generosity to give me years before, when I graduated from high school. Now it was moved into our tiny apartment, where the modern sounds of my compositions sometimes irritated our neighbors.

In my interview at Juilliard, I was seated across from four celebrated American composers. Because of my burgeoning fear of elevators (the newest addition to my increasingly incapacitating list of phobias), I had walked up the stairs. I was out of breath and nervous. I learned that there were only half a dozen available openings in the composition graduate program, and that since my two years in France had resulted in my being one of the older candidates, I was at a clear disadvantage. I mentioned to Vincent Persichetti that as a teenager I had once visited his house outside Philadelphia. He looked perplexed, then brightened. "Oh yes," he said, "you're the one with the mother." (This could have meant many things, but I somehow took it negatively.) I did well when my musical ear was tested. I answered the theoretical and music-historical questions posed relatively well. But I was not admitted. When I tried again the following year, the result was the same. But in the meantime I had at least been studying privately, while working as a teacher myself, and had written a one-act opera to my own libretto, a fable about a princess who marries an owl. Whether I knew that this plot—a kind of transposition of *Swan Lake* with the genders reversed and the nonhuman species changed—expressed something of my own sense of the strangeness of being Mary's twin, I can't recall. What I do remember is the pleasure I had working on the piece, which sounded in places like Bartók's *Bluebeard*. I never got to hear my one-act opera about the Princess and the Owl, but I learned a lot about writing for theater from it. (Coincidentally, my brother's 2008 play *Grasses of a Thousand Colors*, in which the central character marries a cat, explores a similar theme. He tells me that when he wrote it he did not consciously draw the parallel either to the "otherness" of our sister, or to the plot of my early opera libretto.)

I brought the fully orchestrated score of my little opera and the first two—rather dark—movements of a string quartet with me when I applied to the graduate program at Columbia University. This interview process involved two composers quizzing me individually. The first looked at my scores and said to me, "The sooner you break out of this idiom, the better." The second asked me to play through my quartet on the piano. After listening he said that I was "very musical" and "a terrific pianist." I seem to recall that he also mentioned that the word "musical" was out of fashion as a complimentary term at the time, but would make a comeback. (He was right on both points.) Columbia accepted me. Interviewer number two, the composer Jack Beeson, proved to be a wonderful teacher. But studying music composition at a university in those days was a punishing experience. I encountered fierce peer pressure to head in a more "historically relevant" musical direction, regardless of the way I personally actually heard and felt music, and found that while much was said in classes about the theoretical and structural underpinnings of the art, there was precious little guidance about equally important matters, such as how to write gratefully for instruments, or how music's theoretical underpinnings are perceived by the listener.

I entered Columbia with the recuperation of at least some semblance of a musical voice, but then, perhaps inevitably, lost it again. In my first term at Columbia I completed my brooding and fitfully successful String Quartet, and it was performed, opening a window, I felt, onto my actual musical self. But the third and last movement, the one written at Columbia, was the weakest part of the piece. The next two and a half years provided me with an invaluable introduction to many realities of musical life, and to many musicians, some of whom have remained my friends. Yet the studies themselves were unsatisfying and thorny. I could enjoy some of them, but rarely without bleeding. In my composition studies I seemed to be mainly learning how to continue to hold my own impulses at arm's length. Apart from Beeson's, the prevalent pedagogy seemed designed to disassemble music into its component parts and leave the dismembered pieces on the classroom floor. I longed for Boulanger's holistic brilliance.

During my third year at Columbia I became increasingly restive. A valuable class in music analysis introduced me to the mind of the redoubtable theorist, conductor, and composer Jacques-Louis Monod, who like my old teacher Kirchner had been a student of

Arnold Schoenberg. Seeing Monod unfurl a scroll on which he had analyzed every note of an hour-long work by Mahler was deeply humbling, and not a little intimidating. I began composing a twelve-tone chamber piece that I brought to my weekly lessons with Vladimir Ussachevsky, a marvelous composer, who was however suffering from ill health at the time and often seemed distracted in our sessions. Over the Christmas holidays my French girlfriend (now of seven years) told me she was leaving me, and I fell into a deep depression. I couldn't be angry, since I knew that our relationship had long since become essentially platonic. Having even recently resisted her suggestion that we get married, I was in no position to complain. I took long city walks with my chest hurting, feeling as if a dark shroud had been placed over my brain to make me think it was nighttime. That the abrupt separation stirred memories of Mary's long-ago departure seems obvious to me now. But all breakups partake—at least a bit—of death, tearing us from whatever past they take with them, muffling forever the resonances of shared memories and replacing them with stillness and silence.

As I tried to recover from my breakup I wondered whether I was really cut out for relationships. I thought sadly about how this one, which had started so wonderfully, had eventually lost its romantic spark, and I brooded over the idea that sexual desire and love don't always converge, and sometimes seem downright contradictory. Love tends to be singular, and tends toward stasis, whereas simple desire—lust—is profligate and anarchic. I found myself wondering if I would always desire most the women I could never have.

Meanwhile, my brother, who had already written several plays and had been supporting his writing by teaching at an elementary school, working in the Garment District as a messenger and shipping clerk, and making Xerox copies for customers at a copying store, had now backed into a career as a successful actor, almost as if by accident. Having been cast as the comical servant in his own translation of Machiavelli's *The Mandrake*, he now found himself sought after for film roles. When he needed to develop his character as a man attending a divorced men's therapy group in the Burt Reynolds film *Starting Over*, he modeled his character's depressed state on mine.

In the spring I began to go out to dinner with women and to think more positively. I was unused to dating, and was surprised and even amazed that my being so short did not seem to deter many wonderful women from being willing to share a meal with me. I was in therapy at the time and reported to my therapist on one long evening at a very nice, quite comely woman's house, during which she sat across from me on a sofa, stroking her cat meaningfully and discussing opera. I was very flattered that she showed no desire for me to leave, even at past 2 a.m., and I was confused about why I had eventually left. "I guess you didn't find her enthralling," was my therapist's useful observation.

My twelve-tone piece now looked like some foreign object that someone had accidentally left on my desk. While I continued working on it, other ideas for piano came to me spontaneously that I couldn't help writing down in the margins and leftover space of the score. While the ideas were jazzy, formally speaking the pieces weren't really jazz, in that they didn't expand on blues structures but were constructed out of little musical motives, like pieces by Bartók, or Stravinsky's *Piano-Rag-Music*. They were like impressions of jazz—memory pieces. Eventually they began to cohere and to occupy my entire focus, eclipsing the twelve-tone work entirely, and for good. Having overused my critical faculties for so long, I now let loose, for fear of clamping down on something authentic. A few of these new "jazz pieces" were a bit self-indulgent. But what amazed me was that they were not just more vibrant, but also more intelligent, more formally engrossing than the music I had been writing using an intellectual system that didn't reflect the way my mind worked. I brought them to Ussachevsky and he seemed intrigued and entertained. About one of the lyrical pieces he could only comment wryly, "Well, I might have written that for my very first girlfriend, but not after that." (I took this as a negative assessment of the piece, not as a compliment to his first girlfriend.) But at the very least, the set as a whole made him smile. He even went out into the hall and called for Monod to join us and listen to them. Monod seemed to enjoy them too, but afterward averred that "one can listen to all kinds of music for pleasure—Dixieland, for example—but that doesn't mean you should let them influence you when you are composing."

For my part I recognized that I had at least located raw material that had deep roots in my own life—sitting in my parents' living room while my father played the piano and my brother and I played along. The deeper value of these seven "jazz pieces" was not necessarily that they were "jazz," but that they issued from that long-ago untaught self who had desperately needed to speak through music.

In the spring, having decided that I would never be a music professor anyway (a prediction that turned out to be false), I left Columbia, abandoning the doctoral program. My next pieces, for violin and piano, written in the summer, extended this "jazz" voice beyond the jazz realm entirely. While still a bit uncouth, they pointed a way forward. They had some of the directness of the music I had written at the age of thirteen, but were written with a skill and precision that none of my childhood pieces possessed.

Around this time I started going out with a woman I did find enthralling, and whom I eventually married (remaining married to her until our divorce in 2002). We were both at a creative crossroads, she in her literary work, me in my music. At a party at which I had met her for the second time, I played some of my "jazz pieces" and she came and sat next to me on the piano bench. I still remember the thrill of this moment, when a woman I found attractive sat next to me while I played my own music. It seemed so natural to share these particular pieces. When I played them, I almost felt as if I were back at the Friends school, improvising during lunch hour. Coinciding with the beginning of this new relationship something magical happened to my music. I began to bring to bear everything I had learned at school, thorns and all, on the ideas that occurred to me spontaneously. I began to extrapolate a theory from my own ideas, rather than impose a theoretical practice on myself and search for ideas to fit it. I could pick the fruits directly from the tree, but I also knew something about how to make a satisfying pie out of them. So after twenty years of trying to compose, I felt I was finally some kind of composer.

In New York I now led a hectic life, attempting to cobble together a living from playing the piano in shows and teaching at several schools. Eventually I started composing incidental music for theater as well, something I loved doing but which often left me feeling unsatisfied. The experience of being in the theater itself was exhilarating; I adored the actors and being around the phenomenal professionalism of my fellow designers, and I loved having my music used and heard by a general audience. (My favorite project, and the one that gave me the most latitude, was working with director James Lapine, writing the music for his play *Twelve Dreams*, about a girl who kept a diary of disturbing dreams.) As an education in identifying with characters and scenes, coming up with appropriate or paradoxical music for them, or simply carrying out a director's musical wishes; as training in how to write well for instruments, in a range of styles, in concise musical statements, and working quickly—often without a piano—the experience was invaluable. Yet the musical passages required for these situations needed to be both instantly readable and also subservient to the theatrical moment. And in the case of "underscores" they needed to be sonically unobtrusive as well. These restrictions allowed me to hone my craft but also inhibited my ability to discover new things and follow them wherever they led. If something was missing in this milieu it was one of the essential elements that had originally drawn me to music in the first place—the sense that in music I could be free, free to feel whatever I felt and to find out who I was. I realized that I had a talent for doing as I was told, for being "appropriate"—"the easier child," as it were—and for being "incidental." I knew that many artists could wonderfully combine working in the more public and more private artistic spheres, but I felt that there was another layer to life that I could discover only by letting my music follow its own course. I hadn't yet learned enough about what I was capable of doing independently to simply follow what seemed like a possibly promising career path as a theater composer.

For me, composing music had never been about deliberately expressing particular emotions, but about discovering them. I didn't know what I needed to say until I could excavate my inner world by composing.

Surely this need to "discover" came from the lost twinship I so infrequently contemplated, and surely this explains the extraordinary burden I had placed on the whole enterprise of being a composer. Mary's absence had been left largely undiscussed and papered over in our family life. Something essential in me had been papered over too, and music was my one means of access to it.

In these first years of my marriage before I moved to Vermont I said yes to all kinds of projects, feeling that this was the moment to explore as many musical worlds as possible. I wrote music for eight plays, a film, several ballets, and two musical theater pieces—one very tiny (fifteen minutes!), and one including more than an hour of music. I did some orchestrating of other people's music as well, although always with the feeling that others could do it better. I was a good sight reader and seemed to find work easily as a rehearsal pianist. Despite my anxieties, I loved the excitement of being part of a theater band. As an offshoot of this, I played for some jingle recording sessions, and I seemed to do well at that too, in spite of dreading the often claustrophobic recording studios themselves. One orchestrator offered to get me started doing disco arrangements, but I declined the offer, feeling that I wasn't sufficiently steeped in the idiom. Some of the wondrously talented younger people I met during this time went on to successful and lucrative careers in theater, movies, or commercial music. But something nagged at me from inside to write music that tried to explore a more intimate and independent musical world than I could in most collaborative projects. The music that truly satisfied me I wrote on my own time and in my own idiom.

In the early summer of 1983, when I was thirty-five, I was working as a rehearsal pianist for a show that was to open in Central Park in August and, it was hoped, might be successful enough to move to Broadway. (I had already played in two shows that had in fact followed this trajectory.) In July I received an unexpected call from an acquaintance in Bennington, Vermont, inviting me to be a guest composer for a week at the summer chamber music festival there. If I accepted this I would need to be replaced as rehearsal pianist and would forfeit my chance to be a part of the band for the show once it opened. The music director, a composer himself, was aghast that to me the choice was crystal clear. I was being asked to be a guest composer, and I had to go.

This seemingly minor opportunity set in motion the chain of events that led two years later to my moving to Vermont with my wife and our nine-month-old daughter, Annie. I had been resisting my wife's desire to leave the city for some time. But when the connection to Bennington turned into a job offer to teach at the college, I took it. Our son, Harold, was born in Bennington in 1988.

Life in Vermont was wonderful for both our children, and turned out to free me creatively too. Perhaps creating a family and developing some individuality as a composer both required distance from my childhood world. My music lost its self-consciousness. Teaching, and being with younger people, though often exhausting, also turned out to be a great gift, increasingly precious as time passed. Through teaching I continued to learn, and found both a growing connection to the music of the past and to current composers like Toru Takemitsu, Alfred Schnittke, Louis Andriessen, György Kurtág, and others my own age and younger. It almost seemed as if what I had needed more than anything all along was a kind of privacy I would never find in New York. There had been something alarming to me about the praise I received for my work when I was still a teenager not yet ready for it. I needed to protect the fragile inner world my music revealed. It was as if too much public attention to it would mean that it no longer belonged to me, and I would lose my ability to judge it. Distinguishing between this and the "fear of the marketplace" that is the literal meaning of the word "agoraphobia" is beyond my expertise. But I would like to think that I had an instinctive sense of self-preservation that furthered, rather than inhibited, my leading a full life. It is surely true that for obvious reasons I had a horror of appearing to succeed. But I had also always had the barely conscious sense that for my parents my music had the exact opposite function from the one it had for me. For them it was about harmony, about healing what was broken, and about buttressing up a myth of family togetherness and warmth. For me, music was about being released from inhibiting restrictions; about passion, truthfulness, and breaking out. In Vermont no one needed me to stay young or stay inhibited, and I was finally free to grow up. The irony was that the idea of moving away from New York had not been mine, and that I had staunchly resisted it.

Ever since my father's heart attack in late 1971, visits to Mary had become even more arduous for him than ever. He no longer ventured far from Manhattan, and when he made the trip to see his daughter he became gloomy and very anxious, and this worried both him and our mother. In the mid-1980s, not long before he was forcibly retired from his job as editor, a momentous and disastrous change for a man so tied to work and to a job as an outlet for his intellectual and social sides, he stopped going to Delaware altogether. As a result my parents began to invite Mary to Bronxville for yearly birthday lunches in late August. My father was then eighty years old and I was forty. I would come down from Vermont for these events, often with my own family, and when they could, my brother and his girlfriend would join us.

———

From year to year, Mary's recognition of each of us at the lunches never faltered for an instant. Changes of appearance—the advent of glasses, beards, grey hair, baldness—did not seem to surprise her. She always showed an instantaneous, laserlike recognition of our identities. And she could also include new people in her expectations. Once they were introduced to her, she easily accepted my children as part of the family. In the first lunch that included an eight-month-old Annie, Mary seemed jarred by the presence of an unpredictable infant. She looked perturbed when Annie cried, almost as if she felt that her own position as the emotionally volatile member of the group had been usurped. But after that she seemed only to look forward to seeing her. For her part, Annie's encounters with her aunt may have contributed to her desire, many years later, to become a psychologist.

Harold was four years old when he met Mary. His mother and I had prepared him for the occasion by explaining that his aunt was my twin, and therefore exactly my age (then forty-four), but that she was unusual and spoke strangely, and needed to live in a special place for people who had trouble taking care of themselves. As we all sat eating lunch, Mary's focus on the food in front of her was, as always, strikingly serious, as if she were working. She became quiet and plowed through each course with a kind of doggedness. As always, she ate an impressive amount of chicken salad and tomatoes, drank several glasses of iced tea quite quickly, lifting the glass with her pinkie sticking out in her special way, and asked for extra rolls with butter. But her appreciation of dessert was even more obvious. She seemed excited by the ice cream and cake the way only small children are, taking second and third helpings of all three ice-cream flavors (strawberry, chocolate, and vanilla), and occasionally even looking up and smiling broadly with bared teeth to say, "Icecreamandcake." Near the end of the dessert course, Harold said he wanted to go lie down in the bedroom. I went in to see if he was all right, and found him on his back in bed, staring at the ceiling, looking pensive. Harold was and is a thoughtful, philosophical person. "I don't get it," he said to me, as if trying to comprehend the exact nature of Mary's strangeness. "If Aunt Mary is an adult, how come she eats so much ice cream?"

During these visits in Bronxville I finally had a chance to engage Mary in a few activities other than playing the piano in which I could feel the force of her mind operating on its own terms. One was arithmetic. In this technical realm she moves with an automatic smoothness that is astonishing. When I write down many pages of arithmetic problems for her to do, including difficult examples of division involving fractions, or with decimal points, she almost cannot resist completing them. In one dignified and serious motion, she takes the yellow pad and pencil from me without questioning and proceeds to plow through the problems like a farmer riding a tractor over an overgrown field. She does not seem to "do" the math at all. Rather it seems simply a matter of seeing and writing down each answer. And the impulse to complete every page and keep moving through until everything is done seems almost irresistible. Sometimes she mumbles the answers indistinctly to herself, as many of us do performing similar tasks. But, for the most part, the gestures one normally associates with thinking—looking up diagonally while one is figuring something out; placing a finger under a chin for an instant as if needing to steady or freeze the head while it does its work; closing one's eyes to concentrate or to remember—are completely foreign to her. When she was fresh from Sandpiper her answer to each of the proposed arithmetic problems was written in a neat hand, with a check mark placed next to each. As time passed at Briarcliff, this plowing-through-all-of-the-problems style of answering was maintained, but the handwriting became more and more stylized and internal, and her answers became interlaced with the automatic check marks next to them, so one could confirm their correctness only through careful analysis. Nonetheless, they were still always correct, and became, to my mind, a kind of metaphor for all her communications whose meanings must be lost in translation traveling from her brain to the outer world.

Another of her computational talents is counting objects in a box. Again this seems a matter not of counting one by one but of "sizing up" the contents, through the seemingly automatic multiplication of rows of items. If asked to "count" items, she seems almost incapable of *not* doing so, showing none of the temperamental resistance she shows to playing the piano. She will stop and hold herself still and take a brief look. Provided that the objects are in discrete rows, she will offer the result almost instantly, and it is always correct. Whether she knows she is multiplying or does so by instinct I cannot say. But it is as if her brain in motion is frictionless. She shows the same ease and lack of method determining the day of the week on which holidays will fall in the distant future.

However fixed Mary's expectations about our visits were, she always managed to adjust to changes, as long as certain parameters remained constant. For example, there were many indications that as long as there were Reese's Peanut Butter Cups mixed in with the presents of some—any—kind she received, she would be satisfied: she always mentioned "Reese's Peanut Butter Cups" by name, and only "presents" in general; she always reached for them first; and she looked up smilingly, opening her eyes wide, and clasped them happily when she found them, whereas she merely burrowed rather grimly through most of the rest of the items in the bags, with the possible exception of the pads of paper and pens. However, she had learned over time that it was the right thing to do to hold each received item up in the air, grin, and say, "Oooo nice." Overall, she handled the challenge of present opening better than many people I know. (In Gunilla Gerland's masterful memoir of an autistic girlhood, she mentions a similarly treasured item to Mary's "Reese's": a pineapple. As long as a pineapple was included among her gifts, Gerland was completely satisfied by them.)

As Mary matured and her love of sweets became a health issue, she learned that this treasured item could be consumed only one bit at a time, particularly after several generous helpings of ice cream and cake at birthday parties, and she grudgingly adjusted to that too.

I have found notes from Briarcliff taken in the mid-1980s showing that Mary's IQ was again evaluated at that time, and that her doctors felt she had exhibited "stable intellectual functioning over the years." The observers described her as a "small, well nourished woman with brown eyes and short brown hair. She wore glasses and had relatively good eye contact. She manifested a mild tremor in her hands as she worked." From test results they found her to be "severely deficient in skills requiring expressive language, social judgment, and sequencing a logical series of events. The scatter is typical of learning disabilities, as well as retardation, and seems to affect areas related to comprehension and judgment." Additionally they found that "her visual-motor integration abilities are similar to a five-year, seven-month-old child and are slightly below the level expected of her IQ." These notes remind me how hard Mary is to understand.

Each observer over the years has described a somewhat different person. This observer saw her as "a withdrawn woman whose conversation is most often inappropriate. She tends to interact using an echolalic style or repetitive questioning. She reportedly perseverates on issues relating to holidays. In general Mary tends to pass the time rather than enjoy it."

But is this last statement true? Or does the interviewer lack the ability to comprehend the ways in which Mary enjoys things?

Having my own children, helping and watching them as they gradually, bit by bit, learned to crawl, and stand, and walk, and speak, and develop their interests and enthusiasms and characters, stirred profound memories in me of my own childhood with Mary and gave me a firsthand view of the "normal" developmental stages of infancy. My love for my children also somehow made me aware of a deep feeling of incompleteness in myself. I had married and become a parent still trying to fill—or cover over—a void that I didn't even acknowledge to myself. Being a twin was the most basic fact of my life, and the most obvious, yet it wasn't part of my active sense of who I was. To be sure, when asked about my siblings I no longer shied away from quickly establishing the fact that I had an institutionalized twin. But that didn't mean that I understood what I was saying. Like our family's Christmas celebrations in my childhood—which seemed equally heedless of the religious import of the holiday and of the irony of our observing it—my life somehow had a slightly hollow ring to it. In place of Mary herself, I carried a feeling inside me that there was a crucial aspect of my life that I couldn't remember or name.

9

FINDING WORDS

t wasn't until my father became ill in the spring of 1992, when he was eighty-four, that I began to piece together a clearer picture of his romantic life, and of the history of his marriage to my mother. Without my realizing it with any clarity at the time, this process began to allow me to connect my inchoate feelings—feelings that seemed to get expressed only in music—with the things that had happened when I was growing up. It was the beginning of my education about my own life. Presumably, sooner or later this happens to everyone. At first, like actors suddenly thrust out on a stage in costume before sets changed by unseen hands, we just live, we simply "are." Only later, and gradually, do we get to go backstage and learn more—if never enough—about who made the sets and costumes, who planned the show, who conceived the script, built the theater. My "education" continued long after my father's death and is still continuing. But it began with his illness, which forced some of the veils of mystery in our family to be lifted, among them his forty-year-long love relationship with a woman writer at the magazine.

Starting in those months of my father's illness, I began writing down what I was beginning to understand in words, in a diary. You might say that I had been avoiding words, the very center of my father's working life, underestimating their importance, since Mary left the house in 1957. To me, music's "truth" was much more powerful than anything that could be verbalized. And my relationship with Mary was, by necessity, primarily a nonverbal one. Although I didn't even know it, music had kept me close to whatever communications used to pass between us as small children. When I played Beethoven, or the Berg sonata, or focused for long moments on the vibrating messages that seemed to come from between the piano keys as I composed, it was as if I was tuning in to Mary's wavelength. Naturally I only realize this today, in my sixties. I could never have recognized it then.

Yet it turned out that the words spoken to me by my father and mother during the period of his illness were so important to me that I needed to preserve them, lest they be forgotten. There was "truth" here too, and much of it surprised me, even though the basic facts were already known to me. And although it would still be years before I started to think more consciously about Mary's life and learn more about her, what I came to understand during this period was already more than relevant to her story, and therefore to our story. To put it crudely, I discovered that words did matter, but that there were also good reasons I had learned to mistrust them.

My father's "flulike" illness was in fact a small stroke, or perhaps a series of ministrokes. It left him bedridden, his beard unshaven, with a bewildered feeling as if he had experienced a kind of "time out" in his life. For a few days his consciousness had flickered and missed a beat. Afterward he seemed to be in the stunned state one is after unexpectedly fainting, when, reviving to the world, one finds oneself somewhere different from where one had been a moment before, shocked that the world could simply disappear so unexpectedly and then reappear, that time could skip over itself, like a scratched old record. He was frightened and he cried describing his confusion about what had happened to him, saying that he didn't see people on the street with symptoms like his. And in his delicate voice, further frayed by his ordeal, he said, "They made a big mistake making life so short."

After he started to recover he wanted to resume his old routine. His illness had accentuated symptoms that resembled those of Parkinson's disease. He needed to be with the two women in his life, but he was shaky on his feet, having developed the classic Parkinson's shuffling gait, and could leave the house only in the company of an aide and therefore with our mother's agreement, since his entire day was now spent in her care. This precipitated a crisis.

Fifteen years earlier than this, when I was nearly thirty and my brother nearly thirty-five, a friend had finally let slip in my presence the striking—and to a number of people, well-known—fact that while our father spent every night at home with our mother, he divided much of his time between her and another woman. Throughout our childhood and well into our adulthood, our father had managed to maintain a promise to our mother that he would never discuss the subject of his other relationship with "the boys." Only in retrospect did we recognize that although he had never actually lied to us, there were often gaps in his own account of his day. In retrospect I can only recall our mother saying that he had been "at the office" when he hadn't been. I remember her saying such things when, as I now know, they weren't true, and I remember my father saying nothing in such cases, not even words like, "Yes, that's right."

My first knowledge of this complicated life arrangement had come about through a casual comment by a friend who assumed I already knew about it, and thereafter through conversations my brother and I had with my father himself. I had in fact even seen him by chance with his other mate on a few occasions, and had instinctively recognized a depth and comfortableness in their companionship, without suspecting anything more. My father's personality was secretive enough, and his job demanding and complex enough, to account for any mysteries in his behavior. There was already so much that he did that was quite particular to him, and that was left unexplained. As editor, he was as preoccupied as the president of an important nation, and as ready to attend to matters of "state." The magazine was a weekly. There were no weeks when there wasn't an issue to be sent to press, another one to be readied, and many, many more to be loaded with their precious cargo of writing and art. He was always prepared to drop everything to work on a manuscript or discuss an idea. One couldn't easily picture him ever saying to anyone, "This will have to wait. I am on vacation." In fact, one couldn't picture him having a vacation at all, or understanding what the point of a vacation was. If his mind was in fact often on his other family, it was also just as often divided between the here and now and his thinking about the magazine. In the middle of a family meal or while watching the Johnny Carson show, he would suddenly remember things in an issue that needed to be fixed or added, and run to the phone, or he would reach into the inside pocket of his jacket to pull out an envelope and jot down ideas or whole paragraphs. He had hundreds of such envelopes, many completely covered, vertically and horizontally, by his minute handwriting. There were also his many habits stemming from his phobias and sensitivities, all of which I simply thought were normal as a child, but few of which I actually understood. He wore coats and scarves not just past winter but until it was swelteringly hot. He couldn't stand air conditioning. He was finicky about spicy foods, would only eat deboned fish, and was abnormally cautious about exotic dishes. As I later came to do, he avoided elevators, did not take the subway, always sat on the aisle in theaters and public halls, and always near the back. He never boarded an airplane, and he traveled outside Manhattan less and less as he aged. As long as he was editor he was also the discreet confidant of the countless writers and staff and fellow editors who told him of their marriages and affairs, successes and failures, problems, addictions, and breakdowns; he was the repository of as many secrets as any psychiatrist or doctor. All of this is to say that if there were unexplained silences at the dinner table, or if he seemed equivocal in the way he expressed affection to our mother, or if there were gaps in his account of his daily life, these things raised no particular suspicions coming from someone already so full of secrets.

For more than fifteen years my brother and I had known of his other relationship, and also of the child adopted by his other partner, and had made sure that our mother did not know that we knew. His illness changed that. After all the years in which there had been a clear divide in my father's life between one house and another, one family and another, one side of himself and another, he finally felt he had no choice but to call upon his two sons to help him navigate the breach. This meant that he expected us to break the family rule of silence and admit to our mother that we knew about his forty-year romantic entanglement. He was asking us to argue that he had a right to visit his other love. It was a tough decision for us. We had to decide whether to do something that would devastate our mother or disobey our father. He had never in our entire lives asked us for anything, and we feared that he might not have long to live. We also knew that a forty-year "affair" is no longer an "affair" but a way of life agreed to, in some sense, by all involved. We didn't think it was right for our mother to suddenly, at the last moment, prevent him from continuing a way of life she had previously tolerated. With much guilt and trepidation, we complied with his wish and asked her to allow him to resume his visits to his other home, accompanied by an aide.

Not long after this intervention, on our father's birthday, our mother had an attack of colitis that made her bleed so profusely that she had to be taken to the hospital. My brother rode with her in the ambulance, and I followed in my car. Soon we were both seated in the waiting area as she was examined behind a curtain, and we heard her speaking in her melodious and cheerful voice to the young doctors. Our father had insisted on going as well and arrived somewhat later, looking distraught and determined, walking with the young blond female aide who had been helping to take care of him for the past few months. Although he showed no signs of paralysis or other obvious impairments, and had not been formally diagnosed as having had a stroke, it was still obvious, even to him, that he was struggling not only with walking but with other subtle changes in his body and in his mind. I went with him when he needed to go to the men's room and stood guard outside, just as I did with my little son Harold when he went into public restrooms. My father had rarely been in such a squalid bathroom.

The floors were drenched with urine, and the tile walls were decorated from top to bottom with obscene graffiti from spray cans and markers. Since he was a reader by profession, he naturally read the words in front of him. When he emerged, he announced quietly, "Many unpleasant messages." My mother was admitted to a room on the twelfth floor, and soon we were all gathered there as if at a strange family reunion. We were, in fact, in the same hospital where Mary and I had been born forty-four years earlier, and it was the night before our parents' sixty-fourth wedding anniversary.

Our mother's attack was like a delayed cry of pain. On the night we rushed her to the emergency room she was in danger of bleeding to death. But at the hospital her condition quickly stabilized. In the next few days, she remained there in a depleted but alert state, a state of mind from which any remaining layers of pretense had been removed. As a child I had sometimes asked her not to put on her makeup so that I could enjoy her unadorned face. I had always appreciated the solid core of realism and shrewdness that lay beneath her vivacity and girlishness. Here in the hospital she was that natural, unadorned self I admired—relaxed, strong, smart, unsentimental, and beautiful. Now that there was no longer a secret to be upheld, she started to talk frankly to my brother and me about her life with our father. Like a patient being psychoanalyzed, she lay on her back and spoke without self-censorship. She referred to our intervention on our father's behalf as "the day Pandora's box was opened."

Back at the apartment, our father was equally candid. What my parents told me during these days helped me imagine Mary's and my beginnings from their two perspectives.

Piecing their accounts together into one narrative, I could see that, as far back as the 1930s, a period in which psychological "problems" were rarely discussed publically, both my parents had been concealing the more troubling aspects of themselves even from their closest friends. When they were newly married and struggling to find work in New York, my mother had even had a kind of breakdown for which she was hospitalized. At that time she had started to see a psychiatrist, something she told almost no one. Even her sister did not learn about this collapse until sixty years later.

For his part, our father, who had suffered since childhood from his deep fears and serious phobias, had also begun to see a psychiatrist in the late 1940s. The last of five children in a close-knit, boisterous Chicago Jewish family, he had always been the sensitive one. His claustrophobia had begun early. He had confided to his mother at the age of six that he found even being in school confining. He had made it to Europe with our mother for their extended honeymoon in 1928, enduring seasickness on the ocean and probably torment on the train rides through the tunnels of Italy. It was my parents' only trip abroad.

He had loved the *New Yorker* from the time its first issue came out in 1925, but he might never have found himself working there had it not been for a prescient maneuver on our mother's part. When he and our mother first arrived in New York from Chicago, he had in fact gone to the magazine to ask about work in the circulation department, and was turned down. It hadn't even occurred to him to apply as a writer. In the spring of 1933 my parents were so poor that they had to leave their apartment, sell their furniture, and move into cramped basement quarters in a rooming house. Our father spent long hours lying on the bed in despair. Meanwhile, our mother took odd jobs, including one selling greeting cards at a mid-Manhattan store. A friend at the *World-Telegram* suggested that she apply to be tried out as a reporter at the *New Yorker*. She did so and was able to persuade the magazine to give her husband assignments as well. But in fact she never intended to stay there herself, recognizing rightly that our father's gifts would quickly be recognized and that it would be the perfect place for him to work.

Our father probably suffered greatly doing the legwork of a reporter in his early years at the magazine. Though a majestic writer from a stylistic point of view, he was apparently too deeply shy and conflicted to express himself fully as an author under his own name. Quiet and usually constrained in conversation, he seemed to find freedom not in words but in music. A colleague once wrote that at the piano he was "literally a different man." For all the burdens it brought with it, being named managing editor of the magazine during the war years must have also come as a relief, allowing him to assert his views, personality, interests, and immense literary gifts while also remaining hidden. Furthermore, the job allowed him to remain in one safe place, yet without sacrificing the freedom to come and go. Even so, in his private conversation he never let go of the idea that he had accepted becoming an editor out of a sense of obligation, and that it had kept him from pursuing his own writing. He continued to feel this way even during all his years as editor in chief.

I can only assume that he had contradictory impulses about family life as well. He was haunted by romantic longings for a series of beautiful and poetic women. I do not know if he acted on these longings in the first twenty years of his marriage. He was also haunted by a sense of doom—personal, cosmic, and political—and when first married had told our mother that he could not imagine bringing children into such a painful world. But after he had started working as an editor at the *New Yorker* in the early 1940s he changed his mind and suddenly wanted to have a large family. By all accounts my parents were a deeply romantic couple during those years (if clearly "codependent," in today's parlance). At that time they lived only a few blocks from the magazine, and he would often come home from the office during lunch hour and they would make love, hoping to conceive. When my mother became pregnant, they were overjoyed. But that first pregnancy ended in the birth of a baby girl, Wendy, who lived only a single day. Neither of my parents ever saw her. In early 1943 my mother became pregnant again, and in November gave birth to my brother. Not long after, during the height of the war, our mother conceived again. Because of the risk of a miscarriage, she was told to spend the final months of her pregnancy in bed. In the months following Pearl Harbor, New Yorkers were vigilant against possible air attacks. During one air-raid drill, when most people were rushing to shelters in their basements, my father hurried home from the office and got into bed with my mother, telling her that he would rather die with her and their unborn child than survive alone. Sadly, after a seriously premature breech birth delivery, this child was also lost.

In 1946, our father became determined to return to his writing and decided to quit being managing editor of the magazine. There was even a going-away party and a gift of a silver platter on which the writers, artists, and editors had signed their names. But the anticipated liberation was short-lived. After an accident unexpectedly sidelined his successor, he was urgently called back in to work and never left.

My mother conceived again in February 1948. By this time my parents and my brother, in anticipation of a new family member, had moved from Park Avenue South, with its view northward to Grand Central Station, to West End Avenue. I can only assume that since my mother had already lost two children, there was great anguish when she was rushed to the hospital in labor six weeks before her baby's due date. This was surely followed by amazement, relief, as well as continued worry when she gave birth to tiny twins who had to be placed in incubators. But my father told my mother that the birth of the twins was the greatest day of his life. Joy and gratitude after our mother returned from the hospital with Mary and me intact is visible on the faces of both of them in old family photos of the new family grouping, even if my father, who generally flinched from being photographed, still looks characteristically restrained, with a gaze that is somehow both distant and inward.

Their friends showered them with congratulatory cards and telegrams, including this letter from their friend Aimée in Paris, dated September 6, ten days after the twin births:

You can hardly imagine my joy and my surprise . . . Twins! . . . Please let me know immediately how the babies are, even if you just write a few words to tell me so. After the sad experiences you have had, I can't help feeling a little anxious and I want you to tell me if I can be perfectly happy about the news. Things must have been quite unexpected. Wasn't the baby due for October 13th? . . . But where are you going to put all this huge family? How is Wallace and what does he think of all this?

In this context, the gradual realization over the next two years that there was something wrong with Mary must have been, at least for my tormented and fatalistic father, like the confirmation

162

of a kind of curse. Perhaps it contributed to his turning partially away from the family. For her part my mother must have wanted to at all costs deny the problem, if her later personality is any indication of how she would have behaved then. In family photos the toddler Mary is beautiful and delicate and always lovingly dressed. One can imagine how my mother must have relished her femininity. Having already lost one daughter, now there was the danger of having her second taken from her, at least in terms of her life as a normal child, leaving her with two sons and a husband but no fellow female companionship in the family.

In the spring of 1950, the year Mary and I turned two, during the period when Mary's unresponsiveness was first becoming, at least subliminally, a cause for concern, the family moved to a large apartment on the Upper East Side. This was the moment when our father also grew deeply attracted to L.R., who was at the time finishing a major article on Ernest Hemingway for the *New Yorker*. Then, in 1951, Editor in Chief Harold Ross underwent radiation treatments for cancer of the windpipe, eventually succumbing to lung cancer and dying on an operating table in Boston's New England Baptist Hospital in December. At the time of Ross's death my father was particularly attached to his psychiatrist, a Hungarian woman named Dr. Ruth Hanekenda. Shortly thereafter, Hanekenda herself became terminally ill. When she lay dying of lung cancer, Dr. Hanekenda told our mother from her hospital bed that she should loosen her grip on her husband. "There will always be you," she told her. "Don't worry. Even in his dreams, the other women always turn into you. But you must release him a bit." After Ross's and then Hanekenda's death, our father was deeply shaken.

In early 1952, my father was appointed editor of the magazine, a position that channeled his literary gifts and gave scope to his wide mental reach, but also further sealed him off from pursuing his individual creative work. And by this time he had also become involved in the profound additional romantic relationship that continued until his death. Thus, as internal and external pressures on my father accumulated, and at the moment when Mary's disability was starting to emerge, he partially disengaged himself from the grip of his marriage and family life, dividing his romantic self in half. Perhaps this was his way of keeping a window open in his spirit. Now carrying an even heavier responsibility at work, he could at least feel that no one relationship could ever completely claim him. At the same time, his additional love relationship put space between him and the pain emerging in his family life. Whether this divided routine was something that would have occurred in time regardless of what happened at home or at work is an unanswerable question.

Mary and I were then four years old.

At first he kept his double life to himself. It was his new psychiatrist who, seeing how deeply distraught he was about his situation, suggested that he tell his wife that he was involved with another woman. Our father took our mother out to lunch one day in late summer and told her that he was in a relationship that he was trying to get out of. It had to be a horrible moment for both of them. Earlier in the summer our mother had been in a car accident being driven in a cab across the transverse on Ninety-seventh Street. A truck had hit the taxi broadside and left her hanging out onto the street from its left side, with her head bleeding, cuts in her ankles, and two broken ribs. Our father had rushed to the hospital from the office, weeping, and couldn't help making a connection—so he later told her—between the fact that he had betrayed her and the accident. As they faced each other across a restaurant table the day he made his confession, she bore a recent scar from the accident in the shape of a crescent moon on the left side of her forehead. In time it became a faded, delicate white thread, but it never went away, remaining a reminder of the hazards of that summer for the rest of her life.

Thus our mother learned of this catastrophe in her life in 1954. Soon after he had made the initial revelation, our father took a short trip to Boston, during which he tried to decide what he wanted to do. When he returned home, he told our mother that he had no desire for a separation or a divorce, but that he couldn't get over his other woman either. At that time my parents reached an agreement about how he would schedule his daily life to make time for his other relationship but still always spend the night at home, and he agreed that he would not talk to us about it. From 1954 until our father's death in 1992 our mother lived under the strain of attempting to hold together a family in which there was a disabled child and a partially absent husband. For at least a decade or more, she hoped that this relationship would turn out to be temporary and that her husband would indeed "get out of it." At the same time she continued to love him and they continued to love each other, and as far as the evidence indicates, to remain physically intimate with each other, even into old age. For my mother, my father's new love was an aberration, a case of demonic possession rather than an assertion of his own will. And it remained an "aberration" to her even after it became, in effect, permanent. In some ways my father also saw himself as a passive participant in this and other aspects of his routine. When in my early thirties I finally learned of this side of his life and asked him about it, he spoke not so much of decisions he had made but of discoveries. He spoke of finding that there were two women he could not live without. Once he put it quite succinctly: "It turned out that I needed two wives." In our conversations he suggested that he had eventually adjusted to needing and being needed by two households. "It was as if I walked out of the door as one person and walked in the other door as someone else."

This was the marital context in which Mary and I spent our first years, and also the one in which, in 1956, Mary was examined by Dr. Wertheim, and the question of whether or not she should continue living at home was raised. It was a context in which the threat to the survival of the marriage was still new, and in which there were enormous pressures on my parents individually and as a parental pair. I don't believe that these additional pressures caused Mary's institutionalization, but they certainly contributed to the shaky marital environment in which the decisions about her were being made. At the very least they help account for the emotional intensity that both my brother and I sensed beneath the daily surface of things, but that our parents strenuously denied was there. (When my brother urged our parents to go with him when he was returning to see O'Neill's *Long Day's Journey into Night* for a second time, it was because he had seen our own family life somehow mirrored there, and said so.)

In 1956, when my parents contemplated Mary's departure, they clearly hoped that they were sending her somewhere where she would be happier and better understood. They must have also believed that her absence would give my brother and me breathing room. But my mother surely also hoped, deep down, that after Mary was no longer in the house, my father would not need to absent himself so often, or perhaps even at all. She must have hoped, at least unconsciously, that he would no longer need to flee and that his other relationship would finally lose its hold on him. This never happened.

The problem of Mary's sudden departure for me was that it never seemed like a rescue but only a punishment: an expulsion, an exile. To me there was nothing wrong with Mary. She was simply herself, an inextricable part of the world I knew. And because she was almost literally a part of me, I lacked the ability to articulate this to myself, let alone to others. Now that I know something about the brain I understand that such primal things are lodged in the amygdala of the "reptilian brain," the part that simply knows but has no words. While my parents and even my brother were feeling relief and a sense of hopefulness about Mary as she began a new life, I was bereft, wrenched out of wholeness. My sadness and confusion—since after all there was no aura of tragedy, or even of great significance surrounding what had occurred right there in our household—was mixed with an all-engulfing fear. Coincidentally or not, my fear eventually ended up congealing particularly around many things that posed, like this loss, no apparent danger.

According to those who have made studies of twins, like the author Alessandra Piontelli, author of *Twins in the World*, the concept of twins has historically stirred primal fears in many societies, leading to their mistreatment or even murder. Some social groups negatively associate twindom with incest and devise ways to separate twins as infants. However, according to Piontelli, in cultures as different as Indonesia and Ghana, surprisingly, identical twins sometimes end up living together as socially condoned homosexual unions. In at least one culture, fraternal twins are even viewed as ideal mates and are supported in clandestine incestuous marriages.

But even leaving these extreme cases aside, there is a body of evidence suggesting that having a twin creates a special kind of closeness that differs from any other kind, and that the loss of a twin leaves a psychologically unique type of void. In some instances, being a twin is a burden. Some fraternal twins find relief in throwing off the shackles of their twindom as adults and finally separating from a bond that has impinged on their individuality since birth. But Piontelli also discusses the degree to which many fraternal twins who grow up together find it difficult to find the same closeness in their marriages that they already have with their twin, and need to come to terms with the limitations of normal human communication when compared with the instinctive understanding they have already experienced with their sibling.

The connection Mary and I had as young children was unwilled and intuitive. If it can't be deliberately recaptured, it also can't have been eradicated by the passage of time or the absence of shared experiences. Presumably our history as twins is revealed in acts and habits and psychological traits of which we are unaware, and in gestures, like the involuntary tilt of my head I see in photographs. Our early connection, our early unthinking togetherness, like a shadow cast by an unseen sun, simply follows us wherever we are.

Discovering all the buried family history surrounding my earliest years at such a late date in my life was at first a bit like discovering that my parents had been secretly divorced all along and had stayed together for appearances' sake. Yet that description doesn't do justice to the love they still had for each other, or to the complexity of their personalities. Even for me, it would be easy to succumb to the temptation of simplifying their story as one in which an early love gradually grew more distant. But that wouldn't explain the connection, romanticism, and warmth that remained.

No one could say that their rapport was cheerless and cold. Along with my father's indecipherable primness, there was a combination of blushing embarrassment and unmistakable mirth on his face when my mother tried to kiss him in front of us. She was teasing him, and he couldn't help laughing. (She also clearly wanted us to see and remember them kissing.) He may well have been ashamed of the difference in their attitudes toward many things, and in the gaps that had opened between them over the years, but he also seemed simply bashful and protective of their privacy. One of the handful of times I saw him angry at her occurred when she was changing her stockings in front of me, revealing the full length of her plump, shapely legs. The way he scolded her for being heedlessly exhibitionistic suggested jealousy more than parental concern for me. His physical feelings for her seemed very much alive.

I have come to feel that as the crisis in my parents' marriage had solidified into a routine, it also molded itself around their natures, revealing the shapes of their characters and their common talent for compartmentalization. By allowing the currents of his nature to flow freely between two springs, a schism in my father's personality, a venturesomeness buried beneath his tightly controlled exterior, found a permanent outlet. Doubly needed, doubly loved, he was also alone, and therefore free, in a way he would not have been with only one woman. And for my mother, as painful as it surely was to continually contemplate where he was when he was absent, she eventually must have at least recognized that since the routine was permanent, no greater rift than this would ever occur, that in the end she wouldn't lose him; he would always return; he would always come home to her. Strangely—I have come to see—this may have kept her in pursuit of him, in some positive sense, and it may have helped keep her, and her love for him, young.

10

AUTISM

I f growing up with Mary had already taught me to see consciousness as variable, my father's last months drove home the lesson that even the degree and kind of consciousness we are born with cannot be taken for granted as something unalterable. Like our bodies, our minds are on loan to us. Although, thankfully, he never had to deal with dramatically dwindling mental powers, my father did have a terrible neurological scare and seemed to know that it had left him altered. And in his last half year he seemed to be almost literally clinging to his own clarity of mind, fighting off a sense of entrapment and incipient feelings of paranoia. Since writing by hand was becoming arduous, and his handwriting had become almost microscopic, I bought him an electric typewriter. He had always used a traditional one. He tried it out by typing the sentence, "The essence of this machine, and what distinguishes it from other machines, is more than I can understand. It's a beautiful machine, and I think I can learn to use it." The yellow page this was typed on remained in the typewriter until the day he died. He never wrote another sentence on it.

For six months he lived in a somewhat fragile and bewildered state, emotionally vulnerable, but with his mind essentially intact. We talked a great deal during this time, and he seemed deeply grateful that my brother and I did not judge him for the shape his life had taken. After spending so much time in bed, walking was perilous and uncertain. He worried he would never walk normally again. During one of my visits he remarked that "when you see young people in their thirties and forties on the street, they look as if they really expect to live forever." At Thanksgiving he rallied. He was very engaged with his grandchildren and reached out to them. He let Harold, then four, lead him from one room to another. He continued to be intellectually engaged and was fascinated by a book of letters between Hannah Arendt and Karl Jaspers. For a long time he stood leaning on the dining room table, reading them. On December 6, two days before he died, he wrote a number of notes in his characteristic small, delicate handwriting, which, while slightly slanted, was close to normal. Some of these were mailed the day before he died and arrived afterward. One was dated "December 8," another "February 8," a day he did not live to see. In one of them he wrote:

> Thank you for writing to cheer me up. You succeeded in your
> mission as you have so often in the past.

In the wake of my father's death, my mother seemed to finally fully enjoy the fact that my brother and I were now men and no longer "the boys." She particularly enjoyed seeing me in my role as a parent and relished when I would drive her around in my car. She took almost infinite pleasure in seeing my brother's theatrical performances and my musical ones, no matter how strange, disturbing, or outrageous they might be, or how humble the venues in which they were presented. I had always thought of my father as the one who had hankered after a more bohemian lifestyle. But strangely, after he was gone, it was our mother who emerged as unswervingly committed to her son's risky artistic pursuits, regardless of how the products of our imaginations were received or how they fared in the marketplace. She became freer, more accepting, more candid, and, surprisingly, more focused on the future than on the past. Although there were areas of her life over which she maintained the same degree of control that she always had—and Mary was one of them—in many ways she loosened her grip. In 1994 or thereabouts, she laughingly signed a new lease for her apartment that reached past the then unimaginable year 2000. "What a laugh to think that I could possibly still be alive then!" she exclaimed in her characteristically ringing, cheerful voice. She in fact lived until 2005, a few months shy of her hundredth birthday.

After learning so much more about my parents in my father's last days, I had tried to press on trying to understand my past, and particularly Mary, even while moving on with my life, helping raise my children, writing music, and teaching. The experience of writing about my own phobias changed me. By the time I reached the book's end, I felt the loss of Mary's presence in my life more keenly than I had since I was nine years old. It was in my mother's last months that I made my first solo visit to Briarcliff and began to more consciously try to remember Mary's and my first years. In the time elapsed since then, I have tried to visit her more and to understand her better, but always with the dreamlike sensation of trying to understand something that is too fundamental and ingrained in me to be fathomed. When I see Mary, I see a middle-aged woman who is also my own first relation—my relationship of origin, as it were. It is as if I am looking at a scan of my own brain. I see it, but I am also using it to see it. I may have forgotten that I am a twin, but my forgetting is perhaps an expression of the severity of the loss I experienced when Mary left home.

I can't view Mary objectively, and I can't easily capture in words whatever I do understand her to be feeling and experiencing. I do sense, however, that it has made her happy that I have been more of a presence in her life.

Snapshot, 2009: Mary and I are walking to my car in a torrential rain. I am at Briarcliff taking her out to lunch and we are going to meet Katerina. Kat is one of the few people who has really known Mary for a long time as a friend. When she was in her early twenties working as a residential manager at Briarcliff she used to bring Mary to Bronxville and later to New York for her birthday lunches. Katerina, a beautiful woman now in her thirties and the mother of two children, has moved on to be in charge of a large organization. Buffeted by the rain, Mary grips my hand tightly. At first she takes several steps forward and then several back, but eventually she achieves a flow, although it is still slow, hard going getting to the car. "Where's the car?" she says several times, and then "Where's Howard?" several times. Her questions come out in a surprisingly loud, low, intense voice, but in between the questions she also takes short, sudden intakes of breath that give off high piping tones; she also softly sings to herself, as if singing and walking go together. I don't know who Howard is, but I wonder if he drives the van that Mary often takes going out. She has never been in my car before. I show her where my car is up ahead, but that doesn't seem to matter to her. I notice that she seems to take no precautions in the rain and steps directly into the puddles in her running shoes, but always avoids stepping on the grass. Although the water must be physically bothering her, she doesn't actually seem to take any notice of it. She is wearing a stylish black-and-white-striped beret, which matches her grey-black hair, so her head is well covered. Still, I worry that she is getting wet, while she seems only to worry that we aren't staying faithfully on the sidewalk. Once in the car I remind her to put on her seat belt, and she does so very deliberately and deftly. In the mall, we enter the wrong restaurant by mistake—she is again clutching my hand tightly—and encounter a glamorous hostess whose glances from one to the other of us betray faint traces of alarm. Mary is unfazed by my mistake, reenters the car, and this time buckles herself in unprompted.

When we get to the right restaurant Mary has already mentioned several times what she is planning on ordering—pizza and french fries and ice cream—but gradually accepts the fact that there is no ice cream and that there is a nice chocolate dessert, tiramisu, instead. The waitress asks her if she wants any toppings on the pizza, and Mary surprises me by confidently saying, "Pepperoni." I am so used to hearing repetitions that a new word is always startling. Although she never makes eye contact with the waitress, she doesn't let her forget what her order is. When the pizza arrives, Mary says with great authority, "And french fries." The waitress seems surprised by Mary's unusual manner and tone of voice but reasonably understanding. When the fries finally arrive, Mary smiles broadly. Katerina asks her if she wants her to cut up the pizza to make it easier to eat, and Mary says, "Yes, please." During lunch Kat and I sometimes talk with Mary, and sometimes about her. Kat tells me that Mary's comprehension is far beyond what I might think. "But she lives in a black-and-white world, a world of specifics." I remind her that she once had said that I shouldn't feel bad about Mary's life, that Mary might even be the "happiest Shawn." "Yes, that's possible, although I would never say that I can get inside her mind," Kat says. "Still, there are a lot of things that you or I worry about that Mary doesn't think about." That may be, I think to myself, but sometimes her life seems more like an endless process of coping, rather than happiness. I keep wondering about that comment on one of her evaluations from Briarcliff: "Mary tends to pass the time rather than enjoy it." The truth is, of course, that none of us can know what she feels and thinks. At the end of the lunch Mary refers to herself in the first person. She says, "I had a very nice lunch."

My parents seemed to regard Mary as essentially a child throughout her entire life. As her twin, I sometimes think I understand her in some intuitive way that my parents never did, yet in fact my own view of her remains equally blinded. I recognize that she is an unusual woman whose verbal communications are fairly minimal, and whose emotional and social faculties are on a different wavelength from mine. But in a way, in the back of my mind, I can't help thinking of these characteristics as stemming more from choice than from inborn impediments. As a result, I can become disheartened and confused when the sense dawns on me that she will always remain incommunicative.

But I don't think that I am wrong to assume that, since everything in nature has a cause, everything that Mary says and does has a meaning, even if I may never know what that meaning is.

It is no surprise to me that history and geography meant nothing to Mary when they were taught to her at Sandpiper. She seems to lack whatever conceptual grid underpins the ability to generalize about the world or about "life." She experiences firsthand that some places take longer to get to than others, but to go from that personal experience to generalized notions of geographical space, or the concepts of "near" and "far"; to grasp concepts about reality such as "the earth," "continents," "the human race" that cannot be directly experienced and can be learned only through words—this is a huge, and it would seem insurmountable, leap. To some degree, such concepts always need to be taught. If, like Miranda in Shakespeare's *The Tempest*, one were to grow up in isolation on an island ignorant of all beings other than oneself, one's father, Caliban, Ariel, and the spirits of the island, one would need to be taught that there was more to the world than this. But the *ability* to grasp such facts is presumably innate. Even by the age of two most children can draw parallels between their experiences and those of others, and can begin to comprehend that even when the other is not visible, he still exists elsewhere. Mary certainly understands that when someone is "away" she will not see them. But concepts like "real" or "elsewhere" probably mean little to her. The notion that when people are not present or not in communication they are experiencing their own reality elsewhere may be as impossible for her to understand as it is for a six-month-old infant. Likewise, it seems probable that for Mary, as for a child at nursery school, the distinction between whether something is "real" or is only a "story" makes no difference, except when what is real is experienced firsthand. Although over the years she has learned what to expect in her world, this doesn't necessarily mean that she knows what is plausible elsewhere. My assumption is that the class on the geography of earth might just as well be a class on the geography of Middle Earth.

Mary has talents and strengths that are unmistakable—working with numbers (counting, calculations, visualizing the calendar years in advance); retaining and playing music she has heard only one time; maintaining a rock-solid memory for people, things, and routines. She clings to the familiar and the known with an almost ferocious tenacity. Like me when I trace and retrace the same route on a highway until it becomes familiar enough for me to relax about it, when Mary "perseverates" about something new she seems often to be not just repeating what she is told, but confirming it, connecting it to other things she knows, creating links to certainties. I can't help but think that this need for certainty originates in a sense of confusion not unlike mine when I am traveling, the experience of being overwhelmed by impressions and sensations. At the same time, she can also adapt. When there is a change in expectations, she seems to go over the change again and again in her mind until it becomes her new expectation.

Buried in my mother's bureau along with old bills from Gristedes and B. Altman's, photographs, and phone numbers jotted quickly on scraps of paper, I find scattered documents pertaining to Mary.

At the age of eight, not too long before she was sent to Sandpiper, I see that she was examined at length by a child psychologist named Minna M. Genn, a friend and colleague of Herta Wertheim. At that time Genn wrote that Mary was "thought to be an autistic child or a child of atypical development." She wrote that Mary kept repeating the name "Herta" in the waiting room, and that when the doctor was introduced as "Herta's friend," Mary kept repeating, "Herta," "Herta's friend," "Herta's friend, Minna." Genn praised Mary's cooperativeness in taking the test but said that often she could not answer the questions and instead echoed them, "muttered some jargon," or just repeated "one of her perseverative phrases":

> When she failed to respond, it seemed she genuinely did not understand what the examiner was asking of her. But the fact is that in such instances it was as if she was off someplace else altogether and had not even heard what the examiner said to her.
>
> . . . Mary varied between not looking at the examiner at all or poking at her curiously the way a young toddler would do. She seemed to enjoy close physical contact with the examiner and she engaged in some hand-fondling. It was possible to elicit some smiles from Mary by echoing some of the jargon sounds she made.

In the tests she administered she found that Mary's "greatest failure" was "in the area of communication" and that she could perform a number of tasks when they were self-evident or simply required that she imitate what the examiner did, but that she was almost completely unable to follow verbal instructions. Likewise:

> When first given a pencil and asked to draw anything she wanted Mary just scribbled. But when the Bender-Gestalt cards were produced and she was asked to copy them, she surprisingly conformed. [However] she scrawled her copies at random and the only reason that one is separated from another is that the examiner often pointed to the place on the page where Mary should draw.

Similarly she complied with the request to draw human figures. Although some of the details in them seemed at first meaningless, the intention behind these could often be discerned. Overall, though:

> There is a total lack of logic and planning to her work. Mary's perception, as here reflected, is utterly chaotic. She would be unable to pick out from her environment what is salient from what is irrelevant.

In summary, Genn wrote that Mary

> shows many of the earmarks of the autistic child: the failure in communication, the limited interpersonal contact and the perseverative speech. That there may be some organic factors in her disturbance is suggested by a marked disinhibition in motor acts.

The sudden reference to "organic factors" suggests that for Genn, as for many of the clinicians of the time, only impairments in coordination and motor skills were unmistakably organic in origin. The traits in Mary's behavior that suggested autism and perhaps even the low intellectual functioning (which she called "at the margin between a middle-grade and a moderate mental defective level") might possibly be the result of potentially curable emotional problems.

As Jean Itard wrote at the end of the eighteenth century, infants begin life with what seems to be an almost "universal" sensitivity to what is around them, experiencing what he called a kind of "apprenticeship of the senses." They startle at the slightest sound, want to taste and touch and drop to the ground whatever objects they can reach. The toddler's senses "dwell on everything, even on those things which have no connections with his needs." Eventually we learn to sort out the world, putting impressions in a hierarchy. Some senses become increasingly subtle, while others fall away. Every animal's senses are calibrated differently, reflecting their basic needs. One could graph animal senses the way one graphs the overtone waveforms that distinguish the timbres of different musical instruments.

It would appear that from a sensory point of view autistic individuals are often on their own wavelength, either oblivious to some of the impressions that "normal" people prioritize or overwhelmed and unable to tune out or sort through other stimuli that most of us no longer even consciously perceive. It's as if the focusing in the faculties of attention that occurs in the majority of people doesn't happen in the same way in autistic people. But their responses are apparently not consistent even within their own group. Some still startle like infants at loud noises; others, despite being able to hear perfectly well, don't even seem to notice them. The only certainty is that little in the "neurotypical" human environment is designed with autistic people's perceptions in mind.

Gunilla Gerland's writings certainly bear this out, pointing to an underworld of strange sensations and sensitivities that make a kind of logical sense of her responses and quirks and explain her extraordinary need for routine. She conveys what it is like not to have the mental capacity to categorize and contextualize many aspects of experience except in the most limited way. Although as a child she could memorize an entire page from a book at a glance (an ability she shared with Kim Peek, who was the model for the character of the Rain Man in the film of that name), she could never remember faces, and for many years could not comprehend that a person seen in one room was the same person in another room. In fact, she could not understand why people were more important than objects, and in early life was more attached to the back of a living room chair than she was to her parents. Like Grandin, who gives multiple examples in her book *Thinking in Pictures* of the literalness of her mental processes, she grasped meaning only through concrete experience and lacked the ability to follow verbal instructions. She could learn how do things only by doing them, or by having her hand literally guided in the act of doing them.

Gerland details the many kinds of sensitivities and the equally surprising lack of responses that distinguish the inner experiences of autistic people from those of others. She describes her own superior hearing ability in a way that makes it seem akin to the spectacular hearing of dogs and cats. As a child at school this detailed, fine-tuned hearing made it impossible for her to organize sounds into a hierarchy:

> The teacher prattling on was a background to other noises in my ears—the rustle of paper, scraping chairs, coughing. I heard everything. The sounds slid in over each other and merged together.

Gerland experienced woodworking class as a kind of chaotic sonic torture, like listening to ten symphonies played simultaneously at top volume. Yet if she ran from this torture, she was punished by the teacher. Temple Grandin describes a similar agony of confusion in noisy environments.

Many of Kanner's children were reported as living in terror of machines and in particular of their sounds:

> He is afraid of mechanical things; he runs from them. He used to be afraid of my egg beater, is perfectly petrified of my vacuum cleaner.

Hans Asperger similarly catalogued a whole range of sensitivities in his patients in 1943:

> Many children have an abnormally strong dislike of particular tactile sensations, for example, velvet, silk, cotton wool or chalk. They cannot tolerate the roughness of new shirts, or of mended socks. Cutting fingernails is often the cause of tantrums. Washing water too can often be a source of unpleasant sensations and, hence, of unpleasant scenes. In the hospital we have observed hypersensitivity to the throat which was so strong that the daily routine inspection with the spatula became an increasingly difficult procedure. There is hypersensitivity too against noise.

When I think of Mary's attentiveness to food, and remember that my parents first noticed her differentness in the repetitiveness of her habit at six months of "bringing things to her nose to smell," it is tempting to think that she has a particularly acute sense of smell and taste. Itard noticed an "unsurpassable delicacy" in this faculty in Victor, his "Wild Boy of Aveyron," who had a "habit of sniffing at everything that was given to him, even such things as we consider without smell," such as "pebbles and bits of dried wood." Like a dog, he would sometimes recognize those he knew more by smell than by sight. Itard recounts the time Victor lost his way in town and was sought by his governess. Victor didn't recognize her when he saw her out of context, but agreed to follow her home after he had "sniffed at her arms and hands two or three times," at which point he showed his delight in recognizing her.

Grandin conveys the paradox of both craving human touch and being unable to tolerate it. It was not until I read her book *Emergence: Labeled Autistic* at the age of fifty that I recognized that Mary physically resisted being embraced too tightly, and always had.

Our mother was fiercely affectionate—it was practically a matter of principle on her part to embrace almost everyone she encountered, unless there was an unmistakable reason not to—whereas our father exhibited a tendency to avoid physical contact. Out of respect, he gave people plenty of physical room, but he was also overly wary of germs and contagion. Despite his passionate nature, he seemed ill at ease with being physically demonstrative. He carried himself self-protectively in general, and in the company of a group of men—who by and large would tend to be taller and more heavily built than he was—he would look faintly threatened, as if by their very physical proximity. Backslapping or horseplay with men couldn't have been further from his personal style. In the presence of women he always appeared more at ease, and always slightly flushed from the pleasure of their company. But he was still physically restrained.

Our mother had encouraged him to do as his own father apparently had not, and learn to give us hugs and a kiss on the cheek. The hugs he gave in deference to her tended to include a gentle pat on the back, and to have a faintly parodistic character, as if they were given in quotes, with a wink. We didn't really kiss on the cheek. We would offer the tops of our heads for a ceremonial peck.

This was a good idea, and our mother was right to encourage it. But it made it easy to miss that when our sister was offering us the top of her head to be kissed, or slightly resisting a hug that was too vigorous, she wasn't only exhibiting our father's style of affection. Although she frequently gripped one's hand or arm when asking a question and looking at us, and certainly seemed to readily accept her own hand being taken, there was a kind of firmness in her sense of touch that made it seem impersonal and bounded. The kind of kiss on the cheek she seemed to tolerate well is the one she could fully control. Sometimes she would grip our mother's face from the side and carefully plant a kiss there, like a postal clerk canceling a letter.

As Itard does when he tells in his *Mémoire* of Victor's lack of response when a rifle was fired right next to his ear, many have noted that autistic individuals can sometimes be *hypo*sensitive (have an abnormal lack of sensitivity to some things) as well as *hyper*sensitive. Gerland goes into detail about her visual deficits and unreliable sense of space. Writing about how her sight becomes compromised in the dark, she says that

> my eyes never got used to it. As it grew darker, everything just got greyer until it was like looking at a television after the programmes were over—a kind of gravely grey darkness that made me lose all sense of direction.

Gerland also describes physical sensations that would be impossible for most of us to imagine:

All the time I was growing up, I suffered from an almost constant shudder down my spine. Periodically, the shuddering grew worse, while at other times it kept relatively quiet so that I was able to live with it. It was like that feeling the moment before you sneeze, only as if it had got stuck and was suspended inside my spinal cord in order to turn into something permanent.

Despite her early discovery of reading, and her photographic memory for the visual image of each page in a book, she had always struggled to vocalize words. This struggle caused her to compulsively make "a sound half-way between clearing my throat and swallowing":

> When I didn't succeed in connecting with my nervous system so as to make my voice carry out the order to speak that I had given it, I felt as if my voice had disappeared. I worried that someday I wouldn't have a voice at all . . . so I made that sound all the time. I did it to reassure myself that my voice was still there.

––––

Autism subsumes aspects of obsessive-compulsive disorder. Autistic people can't help repeating actions—motions like rocking back and forth, spinning, or hand-flapping—or repeating spoken phrases and sounds, and they are prone to more general obsessive preoccupations: with food, with trains, with numbers. Mary is clearly preoccupied with food, and with holidays, and with maintaining a grip on what to expect in her immediate world. At the same time she has a number of repetitive physical habits that amount to tiny rituals, although the rocking I remember from infancy, and which is so common in autistic people, is not one of these. When she walks, she often counts her steps and then repeats them. Sometimes she walks three steps and then taps the wall three times. She also seems to have a similar counting system for drinking from the water fountain.

Long ago Darwin observed that the physical expressions of emotions in humans tend to be remnants of evolutionarily adaptive bodily movements. The open mouth and widened eyes of astonishment, for example, derive from our need to take in as much oxygen and see as much as possible when surprised by a threat. Our involuntary physical behaviors are therefore deep indices of our states of mind and body. In animals seemingly useless unusual repetitive behaviors (called "stereotypies") are associated with distress and confinement. Tigers, leopards, and elephants pace in the confinement of zoo cages; many animals groom compulsively when they are hungry or anxious. The list of such behaviors in animals is a long one. One theory about the physical stereotypies of autistic people is that such behaviors are necessary to restore their sense of physical equilibrium, compensating for an inner restlessness and chaos so intense that it can be assuaged only by a regular outward motion as soothing and hypnotic as the rocking of a crib.

Perhaps the same type of origin lies behind their more general preoccupations. Oliver Sacks, in a video on autism entitled "Rage for Order," discussing the universal human need to make the potentially infinite complexity of reality manageable, distinguishes between the average person's gradual discovery of "an order in the world" with the autistic need to impose a system of "private ordering" upon it. "We all have to make sense of the world," he comments, "in order to make [it] intelligible, communicable, and bearable." For autistic individuals this can entail elaborate routines and rituals that seem to fulfill the function that work, hobbies, or pastimes do in the non-autistic. These routines are extraordinarily individualized and varied, and all the more mystifying when unaccompanied by any verbal explanation. Some of them overlap with the routines of collectors and enthusiasts. For example, one of Kanner's patients became obsessed with *Time* magazine covers and amassed a complete collection of them in chronological order. In many autistic people, the need to repeat seems to dovetail with an extraordinary sense of—and memory for—organizational patterns.

In the Oliver Sacks film, a boy is seen viewing the same portion of a video again and again, always stopping the remote control at the same frozen image of a girl's face. The boy himself recognizes the strangeness of performing this ritual every day for many hours, and cannot explain it. A young Indian boy who is unable to speak finds a "haven in the world of numbers," and hums while filling endless sheets of paper with complex mathematical problems that he solves effortlessly. His paintings of star constellations are astronomically correct.

The twelve-year-old autistic child Elly Park, who was the subject of a number of books and studies by her parents, Professor David Park and his wife, Clara Claiborne Park, devised a complex unified system combining prime numbers, the exact position of the sun and the moon and the number of clouds in the sky on a given day, her own experiences from that day, and other elements real and imagined into a way of organizing her moods and the rules she followed for eating. (For example, the exact level of juice that she put in her glass on a particular day would depend on the character assigned to that day.) She had her own language for days, which included twenty-nine varieties of them (twenty-three actual and six fictitious), and her own way of calculating which type of day it was. Names for days included "daynothing," to "daydarkcloud," to "dayhighplacemusic." All of this had a great inner consistency but would have appeared to be totally arbitrary even to an attentive observer. Were it not for the fact that Elly's parents studied her behavior systematically from her early childhood on, and that her father was a physicist who had the mathematical skills needed to decode the highly complex computations Elly was able to do spontaneously in her head, no one would know of the system at all.

Park's study includes an anecdote describing an incident when an unsuspecting dinner guest reached for his salad portion before Elly did and was met with screams and tears that lasted for half an hour. The guest did not know that the salad had been prepared according to Elly's specifications and she needed to be the first to dip into it, when the numbers of ingredients were still exactly right. Because of their study, the Parks knew that behind what would have appeared to most people to be a meaningless tantrum was a hidden mathematical logic. Indeed, to mentally reverse the damage and restore mathematical order, Elly soothed herself by performing a progressive series of multiplications and divisions, culminating in

$$5300530$$
$$37 \overline{)196119610}$$
$$37 \overline{)7256425570}$$

The Parks saved her work and devote a page to explaining the mathematical significance of the operations she performed.

Elly invented different systems at different points in her life. Once in place they would dominate her moods and actions and, seemingly, her thoughts. New systems replaced old ones as she aged. Her excitement about numbers started suddenly at the age of twelve after her mother had taught her about fractions. Elly soon became adept at factorization. She also assigned individual names and characters to a set of some forty integers of various sizes from small to very large (7,256,425,570). On the one hand, there were numbers that created so much happiness that she would not pronounce their names; on the other hand, there were the "bad" numbers, like the number 75, which, if seen on a license plate, received a swift kick. What is doubly remarkable in all of this is that Elly suffered from extreme aphasia: speaking intelligibly at all was usually extremely difficult and painful for her. Yet she was visibly pleased to be asked about her "day" system. The first explanations she gave about it at age twelve were amplified in later years when her speech had improved and she had moved on to other preoccupations. The Parks write of Elly's "wide swings of emotion as the sun came and went," and "the trembling excitement" with which she filled her glass in the morning; they describe her running from window to window following the trail of the light of the moon and the shadows it cast, and her tears when it disappeared behind a cloud. (The moon, which she assigned the number 7, was too exciting to be referred to by name; she would only call it "something behind the tree.") "It is clear," they write, that "many of the actions of people around her, and most of their interests and concerns, have no meaning for her at all. It is our conjecture that the system . . . represents Elly's effort to fill the deficiency by establishing her own kind of meaning."

Not everyone in the autistic category necessarily organizes the world in such an intricate way. A thirty-one-year-old autistic man named Jerry, who had been diagnosed first by Kanner and later by the same doctor who diagnosed Mary, Dr. William Langford, was interviewed in the late 1970s around the time that he had secured a job, one that required only computation and a minimum of human interaction. He is described in a 1979 article as having an outward manner that was uniformly flat, exhibiting no outward sign that he had the kind of rich inner life described in Elly Park's case. He recalled a childhood of "confusion and terror" in which the unpredictability and strangeness of human behavior—indeed the behavior of any living creature—made most of the activities of daily life unbearable. He had learned to speak at the age of three, and when he did he spoke volubly, but only to himself, and rarely to communicate. At age four he found solace in spinning objects and in copying out articles from the newspaper, or copying the labels found on boxes and cans. He had an extraordinary memory and would recite to himself long lists of the prices of grocery items he remembered. At age five his drawings were entirely of clocks and radios. He was extraordinarily sensitive to sounds and smells. He demanded a level of consistent order in the family home that made his parents and brother feel tyrannized, and this resulted in his being sent to an institution at the age of ten. At the institution, he was most content doing arithmetic or looking at maps by himself. When he returned home at the age of twelve he attempted to participate in school life but was a social outcast. As a grown man, he continued to be taken care of by his mother, and he remained a creature of routine. It took him two hours to take a shower "because he has to place the nozzle, bath mat, curtain, etc. in an exact relationship and then wash in a prescribed manner." Nevertheless, his social skills had improved to the degree that he could hold down a job.

Kanner's insight was to suggest that autistic individuals like

Jerry feel everything beyond their obsessive activities to be an *intrusion*, a lapse from what Sacks would call their "haven" of order. But the exact nature of each person's ordering of life is unique, and the origins of it generally remain an unsolved puzzle.

Presumably, Mary has never been a puzzle to herself. Even with all the suffering she has experienced, there is never a sign that she wishes she were different than she is, or that she has the concept that there is a way of being human that is considered "normal," and that those who are "normal" find her "abnormal." Gunilla Gerland's memoir of growing up, *A Real Person*, takes its title from her childhood wish that she could experience the world the way others did, and therefore behave more like them and finally be accepted and no longer routinely abused. Having grown up lacking an intuitive grasp of many things that others took for granted, and suffering from sensitivities that others appeared not to have, she longed to be "a real person." Despite her struggles with speech, she was innately highly verbal. Ultimately it was the written word that rescued her. Until her midtwenties, when she read a description of people exhibiting autistic features in a book she found at the library, no doctor, including her own therapist, had ever considered her problem to be neurological. After her discovery of the concept of autism led her to seek out a child psychologist who was an expert in this field, and she was finally diagnosed (as "a woman with high functioning autism"), she finally gained enough perspective on her own marginalized state to begin to emerge from her profound depression. With her new understanding, her communication skills improved, and she began to participate effectively in the human world, eventually even becoming an author and lecturer on the subject of autism.

Mary appears to lack Gerland's verbal talents. Yet Gerland was herself almost entirely noncommunicative in her first years. What if Mary had stayed at home or been able to remain at Sandpiper permanently? Would her ability to communicate have improved? In the absence of her own account of her experience, how can one begin to "diagnose" her? How can one ever comprehend the way in which she is whole, and human, despite her handicaps?

IQ and comprehension tests appear to reveal the limits of Mary's understanding and place her abilities in the verbal and math realms somewhere at the elementary school level—or, technically, in the "mildly retarded category." But given her social and communication limitations, can one be sure that these tests have actually registered the limits of her "intellectual" potential? When Mary withdraws into quietude or lashes out in distress or talks to herself—what is happening to her? Is she psychotic in addition to being autistic? Is she in some kind of physical pain? Is she overwhelmed by bizarre sensations and responses that she cannot verbalize? How can her unknowable inner life be evaluated in order to determine whether she is "imagining" things that bother her—suggesting psychosis, hallucinations—or simply responding to cues that the more neurologically "normal" do not perceive? And in any case, where does one draw the line between unique personality traits and "mental illness"? Who can say if she would function "normally" were it not for the one underlying condition called—at this stage of medical history—"autism"? As everyone on the "autistic spectrum" seems to, Mary has a vigilant "need for sameness." But is this part of her "autism" or just an exaggerated version of a family trait that a glance at the routines of her parents and her two brothers would reveal to be a shared tendency? Or is it both—a deeper defect in whatever genetic characteristic underlies the "need for sameness" in the rest of us?

In my mother's things are notes from an early psychological examination of Mary at Briarcliff, containing the following observations:

1. Impulsive, aggressive behavior: entered office, sat in swivel chair, tried to open brief case.
2. Repetitive, primitive demand for food (although 10:30 a.m.), with very little tolerance for frustration. Agitation and "frenzied" responses, difficult to assuage.
3. Bizarre and inappropriate rituals: kissing right arm, pinching right arm.

It is hard to detect any "aggression" in the behaviors listed in the first observation. If given a choice of places to sit, many of us would surely choose the chair that looked most comfortable or most interesting to sit in. We can assume that Mary failed to recognize that she didn't have a choice. The curiosity shown in her trying to open the briefcase seems to show where her interest and attention went—(i.e., not to the interviewer). For a toddler in her shoes, trying to open the briefcase would be considered entirely "normal." Rather than simply saying that her behavior was impulsive, why not say that her behavior was, in this respect, not unlike that of a curious small child? For a grown woman to act this way may be atypical and incongruous, but it isn't aggressive or particularly impulsive.

Anyone who has raised a child recognizes the infant in Mary's "primitive demand for food . . . with very little tolerance for frustration." Unlike an infant, who only has a language of sounds and cries with which to telegraph distress, Mary had learned the language of demanding food, had learned to expect meals at regular times, and had learned how to be patient by the age that this interview took place. But she had also learned that treats could be provided at unexpected moments and could sometimes be offered to soothe her when she was upset. Perhaps, like anyone else in a strange environment or stressful situation, she would have reached for a cigarette, or a stick of gum, or a cup of coffee, had she had the independence of the average adult. Perhaps she asked for food as a way to cope with the stress caused by the interview itself.

Or possibly it was only one of her repetitious anticipations of food to come ("Peanutbutterandjellysandwichesforlunch"), and her "frustration" resulted from the fact that the interviewer, not knowing her personal routines, didn't confirm the lunch menu. In any case, how could the interviewer tell the difference between her routine behavior and the way she was acting in that particular situation?

What is the significance of Mary's kissing and pinching her right arm? Doesn't this "bizarre" activity have to have some cause? Could it be a response to a strange physical sensation like the ones Gerland describes? Or is it perhaps some habitual coping device, replicating a moment from long ago of feeling pain and then a soothing maternal kiss?

During the period when Mary and I were young, autism was considered a condition of childhood. When children diagnosed with "infantile autism" grew up, they were then diagnosed as "schizophrenic." In fact, Mary's diagnosis came to encompass aspects of schizophrenia around 1966, at the time of her admission to Briarcliff, when her behavior was being viewed as increasingly volatile.

In the next decade, medication to control her more tormented states was gradually increased. By 1976, she was placed on two antipsychotic medications, Stelazine and Thorazine. At this point, her diagnosis read, "There are various designations, from autism, to psychosis, to mild mental retardation with prematurity." The addition of "psychosis" can be linked to the second point under observations: "Severe discordant behavior: hallucinations, screaming, biting, as described." Still later in her treatment she was placed on Haldol. Eventually Haldol was replaced by risperidone. All these drugs carried risks, including the risk of creating what is called tardive dyskinesia—involuntary, jerky movements, usually of facial muscles, that become permanent, even if the medication is discontinued. With risperidone, this risk is significantly lowered.

If a person is schizophrenic, they are, by definition, subject to imaginings. But distinguishing between responses to stimuli in the outside world and responses to an imagined reality is not simple when one is dealing with someone of unusual sensitivities. The first winter Mary was put on antipsychotic medications was a very cold and snowy one. Clients at Briarcliff spent an unusually long time indoors. This changed Mary's living conditions and could have created external stimuli that upset her. Mary was very disturbed that winter. There were worries about her tendency to self-injury—her compulsive biting of her arm and habit of tightening strings around her fingers until there was a risk of losing circulation in them. She would also sometimes stuff things inside her vagina. But how an observer could determine that she was suffering from visual or oral hallucinations is hard to imagine. In a case like this one, where there was an unexpected change in social and living conditions, what could look like psychosis from the outside could have its own internal logic. In my conversations with Dr. Trombly, he has tended to agree with me that "schizo-affective disorder" may indeed not be the right description for the condition underlying Mary's outbursts and mood swings—that quite possibly her sudden bursts of alarm or anxiety are logically connected to reality, set off by elements in the environment that other people would not notice. This noticing is, in a sense, an untapped gift, and will no doubt remain so.

I speak with Dr. Alexander Westphal, a New Haven–based child and adolescent psychiatrist whose focus is individuals with autism spectrum disorders. He tells me about the work of his colleagues Drs. Ami Klin and Warren Jones of the Yale Child Study Center. Klin and Jones have studied what engages the visual attention of autistic individuals as they watch naturalistic scenes by using films ranging from *The Red Balloon* to *Who's Afraid of Virginia Woolf?* and eye-tracking equipment. "This work suggests that it may be no exaggeration to say that they see an entirely different world than the one neurotypicals see," Westphal tells me. "For example, while watching *Who's Afraid of Virginia Woolf?* a 'normal' person might focus on the way in which the characters interact with one other, watching eyes, following head gestures, etcetera. On the other hand, a subject with autism might miss this information entirely, concentrating on doorknobs, on the rich background detail in the film. The powerful point that this research makes," Westphal continues, "is that the world of a child with autism may early on be built around such things, and the ultimate phenomenology of autism may result from the cumulative effects of this . . . a developmental trajectory oriented away from the social and leading to, in Klin's words, an entirely different 'topology of salience.' If this were the case it would suggest that early and aggressive intervention focused on reinforcing social cues might be effective."

I ask him about whether the bewildering array of therapies offered to autistic people today are effective. "Well, some are unproven and potentially extremely dangerous, including chelation therapies and steroids. Others, like ABA (applied behavioral analysis), can be effective in getting children to learn to interact socially. But these insistent repetitive drills can be difficult to watch: 'Look in my eye, Johnny. Nice work.'—again and again. It is a kind of intensive manners training, and it is grueling because the goal may not make sense for the children. It simply isn't intuitive for them; it is not in their natures to look you in the eye."

I tell Westphal that I often wonder what my childhood would have been like if Mary had remained in New York. In the period of my childhood there were no "support groups" for families with mentally disabled members. There were very few "group homes" for the retarded. There were few options for parents of children with problems as severe as Mary's, other than institutionalization. He agrees that now it is different, in that funds for running a place like Briarcliff have dried up and been moved to home-based settings where residents live perhaps six to a house and are chaperoned by one or two staff. The content of their days might be similar in many ways to Mary's, but they live within normal communities rather than in private enclaves. Westphal also adds that, as is the case with cancer and other illnesses, there was a layer of shame and embarrassment surrounding the problem of having a disabled child in the 1950s that has certainly diminished in our time.

My friend Betsy Blachly, who is a teacher in early childhood education and also works with autistic children as a music therapist in New York City, agrees that the world is beginning to catch up with the problems of disabled people of all kinds. "In the 1950s, practically the only model that existed was that of sending the child away. Today if you have a baby with a need in this country, there are instantly places you can go to get services that help you. This is now the law. If a baby is born without an arm you can get someone to come to your house to work with her to teach her how to learn to sit up and take care of herself. If one has an autistic child there are agencies who can send helpers to come to your home to do physical therapy, speech therapy, occupational therapy, and to provide counseling for the family. Your pediatrician will help you apply for services." She tells me that among the many challenges for parents of autistic children is to find the activities that make their children happy, where they are relatively at peace. "At bottom that's why I do music therapy. One of the autistic children I work with is on lithium. She has obsessive-compulsive issues, which the medication balances. So many things in her life are out of kilter. Going to school on the school bus is so difficult; being at the school itself is so difficult. But she is so contented doing music. She sings and makes up narratives about invented characters. When she is making music the world is not off kilter for her."

Dr. Westphal reaffirms what a toll having such children can take on families, siblings included, and notes that parental conflicts over how to handle mentally disabled children, particularly when they are aggressive, paranoid, or violent, have often destroyed marriages. I am awestruck that, even in the time of my childhood, there were families that had the love, fortitude, and resourcefulness to incorporate such children into their world, rather than consign them to a separate one. It is entirely possible that Mary was better off at Sandpiper and Briarcliff than she could ever have been in New York City. But in any case, leaving that question aside, only a more naturally unified and self-sacrificing family than ours could have tolerated the enormous challenge of bringing her up at home. Given their own psychological fragility, the pressures on their marriage, and their fearfulness that Mary's fate would engulf the lives of their sons, it doesn't surprise me that my parents made the choice they did. In order for us to have remained intact as a family of five, we would all have had to accept and embrace Mary's world as a part of our own. We would have had to become even more like her than we already were, and to recognize her in ourselves, and we would have had to build our family life around her.

My challenge now, in my own later stage of life, is similar. Can I allow myself to feel once again that Mary is a part of me and that I am a part of her? In his marvelous book *A Healing Family*, Japanese author Kenzaburo Oe writes of his life with his autistic son, Hikari. Comparing the reactions of those who are suddenly disabled as a result of an accident to those of a family dealing with a family member mentally disabled since birth, he explains that in the second case it is not the disabled person but the family itself that must pass through painful stages of adjustment: from shock, to denial, to confusion, and ultimately, after much effort, perhaps to acceptance:

> I have had to learn through concrete experience to answer such questions as how a handicapped person and his family can survive the shock, denial, and confusion phases and learn to live with each of those particular kinds of pain. I then had to find out how we could move beyond this to a more positive adjustment, before finally reaching our own "acceptance

phase"—in effect coming to accept ourselves as handicapped, as the family of a handicapped person.

For Oe, the process that he went through, first by resisting the urge to flee from his family when his son was born, then to agree to surgeries for his son, to learn to live with him and include him in his own daily life, constituted the enactment of an attitude that he believes society at large should have. As much as possible, he favors the integration of the handicapped back into society:

> On a . . . personal level, I can imagine a very concrete example of what happens to a society that shuts out its disabled by asking myself how we ourselves—the Oes—would have turned out if we hadn't made Hikari an indispensable part of our family. I imagine a cheerless house where cold drafts blow through the gaps left by his absence; and, after his exclusion, a family whose bonds grow weaker and weaker. In our case, I know it was *only* by virtue of having included Hikari in the family that we actually managed to weather our various crises.

———

Our mother's last few years, like moments in our father's last months, seemed once again to illustrate the fragility of the human mind. Her decline began physically, with osteoporosis and difficulty walking. As she passed the age of ninety she became increasingly hunched when she stood up and was no longer secure on her feet when she took her short, windblown walks down Fifth Avenue. Once she even fell over onto the pavement and needed to be helped up by passersby. Eventually she needed to support herself with an old cart on wheels even when walking down the halls of her apartment. She insisted on continuing to live by herself and doing much of her own cooking, and did so until the day she tried to reach an object on an upper closet shelf and suddenly felt that she couldn't move her legs at all. After that she finally agreed to obtaining a walker and to having someone live with her and look after her, a prospect she had previously called a "nightmare."

It wasn't too long before she spent much of the day in a wheelchair, with periodic visits from a physical therapist who exercised her legs in the hope that she could regain motion in them. After a time she could not feed herself. For a few years, even as her hearing deteriorated, her mind remained sharp. She was handed the newspapers and read them daily. She watched the nightly news and reacted with characteristically trenchant observations. But she was terribly depressed. She didn't want to be seen in her wheelchair and preferred not to be taken outside. Eventually she didn't even want to look out the window. However, she still wanted to spend a part of the summer in a rented house in Bronxville, which she had always loved. In the summer of 2000, while there with an aide and a family friend, she had her first seizure. Medics were called who intubated her. In Vermont I got a call from the hospital saying that she was in intensive care, unconscious and with a collapsed lung, following a stroke.

I drove there as if in one unbroken, hypnotized motion, as I had when my son Harold suffered a concussion in a skiing accident far away, and when I heard that my father had died. As phobic as I am about traveling, there are moments when I don't actually even register that I am in a car. In this particular instance it was as if the car itself took on the emotional strain of the moment. By the time I had reached the hospital, smoke was pouring out of the hood and it needed a week's worth of repairs.

I was at my mother's bedside for two weeks. She lay unconscious with her lungs connected to an oxygen tank for several days. While she lay there, in a kind of purgatory, she seemed to me to be the most precious creature alive. Gradually she revived, and survived.

Meanwhile, my brother had been stranded—bound by contract—on a movie set in Australia, desperate for news, and distraught at the thought that our mother might not live until his return.

Once back in New York, our mother seemed at first almost her old self. In fact, she had even recovered her former high spirits, frequently asking to be wheeled to the window to look at the boxes of azaleas she had long ago hung outside the windowsills, and over them, to the trees in Central Park. She no longer minded being seen in a wheelchair. When I was able to come down to the city we would go to concerts and ballets together, and we would place her wheelchair on the aisle. She even attended some of my performances that way, as well as some of my brother's plays. We took her to memorial services for her friends, where she remembered everyone she saw.

After her hospitalization I had started to call her every night. As the weeks and months passed, I continued to call every night, even after she had lost the ability to engage in a real conversation. Sometime in the year 2000 she started to panic, sensing that her mind was losing its grip. She complained that she felt she was "going mad." By late in 2001 the fear had passed, but she did not always seem to recognize people. There were moments during my visits with her when she called me "Bill." She spoke less and less.

She did not seem to be reading when the newspaper was placed in front of her. On the phone when I said, "I love you," she would answer, "I know you do," and her voice would trail off. There was a moment when I suddenly realized that Mary was now much more verbal and interactive than our mother was. By 2003, she could still hold the phone and listen, and, according to those with her in New York, her eyes would widen and brighten as I talked, but she could not answer at all. I still continued these one-sided conversations every night.

My parents had always maintained that it would upset or even completely unhinge Mary to return to the apartment in New York where she spent her first eight years, even if only for a two-hour lunch. Therefore, while my brother and I kept organizing the yearly lunch routine with Mary even after our mother couldn't go to Bronxville anymore, and even after our mother's health and mental sharpness had markedly declined, to do this we brought everyone, our mother included, to a room in a hotel for two hours and had the hotel prepare the exact menu we had always made in Bronxville.

But by the summer of 2005, our mother, now ninety-nine years old, was unable to move her hands or legs, to take care of herself in any way, or be easily transported out of her apartment. She had not spoken for many months and would open her eyes only for a few minutes at a time. It had been several years since she had shown unmistakable signs of knowing what period of her life she was living in. She would sleep for much of the day, reviving intermittently for brief glimpses of daylight. At these moments one felt that, even if a lot of specific knowledge had escaped her, she still did know whom she knew and whom she loved best, and she could still smile with her eyes. One felt that in some amazing way, her personality was intact. Our friends Amy and Piergiorgio were now living with her and, along with an extraordinary woman named Marjorie, helping to take care of her. Piergiorgio prepared wonderful soft dishes for her that she was fed while her eyes remained for the most part closed. Amy read to her, and she seemed to stay awake longer when this was happening, listening in her darkness, in a kind of suspended state of alertness. Words still seemed to reach her and to interest her.

But taking our mother to a hotel visit with Mary in this state seemed impossible, and at this late date it finally seemed sheer insanity not to risk bringing Mary to the apartment in the interest of our mother and Mary having a last chance to see each other. Together, Amy, Piergiorgio, Marjorie, my brother, his girlfriend, and I decided to organize a lunch for Mary there. We were worried about whether she would be shocked to see her mother in such a passive state in her wheelchair—unable to talk with her or hug her, and possibly remaining asleep—and we were equally concerned that she might suddenly explode in some kind of blind fury at the sight of the apartment that she hadn't seen since the age of eight.

Mary is certainly a creature of routine. Even moving her across the hall in her dorm at Briarcliff required a lot of planning. She seems to outdistance even the other members of her immediate family, all of whom could be described as attached to predictability and for the most part risk-aversive, in this respect. She has always seemed to set her inner clock to the expectation of the impending events and holidays she anticipates so vividly on the calendar. Yet it also appears almost as if the passage of time has no particular meaning to her. In anticipating her birthday lunches she always seemed to be both excited and yet also to expect a repetition of what had happened before. In anticipating the birthday lunches my parents planned for her, she would always reel off the menu she was expecting: chicken salad, tomatoes, rolls with butter, iced tea, ice cream, and cake. Mary has a way of speaking that can almost be like singing or intoning, with each syllable being given enormous weight. This menu list always sounded particularly emphatic. When she would arrive at the Bronxville house she would always mention the food again. During the chicken salad course, she would often look up and mention a few times that ice cream and cake were coming later.

Anticipating her arrival, I racked my brains for the precise lunch items we needed—the exact type of rolls, for example. Amy mentioned the upcoming lunch to our mother every day, whispering in her ear. I purchased a birthday cake and ice cream; my brother bought presents; Marjorie brought balloons. At the last moment, in addition to the chicken salad and tomatoes and rolls prepared by Amy, Piergiorgio decided to cook some of his Italian specialties, and Marjorie prepared a huge watermelon with sliced fruits inside and an elaborate pasta salad. These dishes looked as startling to me in this context as a pork loin at a seder—but it was too late to worry.

Mary arrived at the door of the apartment with her escort from Delaware. She had a particularly comfortable, confident air. In fact, it was as if she knew her way around. Later we all tried to remember if she had asked where the bathroom was or had simply gone to it out of long-buried habit. But regardless, her comfort in the apartment, and with her mother, was self-evident. But this was the least of the surprises. At the lunch table she ate her helpings of chicken salad and rolls and tomatoes, to be sure, but she was particularly taken with the antipasto, which she asked for second and third helpings of, while asking for more of each by name. She dug

into the watermelon and fruit and the pasta salad with obvious
delight and interest. When she is eating, it appears to be very much
the focus of her attention, and she doesn't like to be distracted by
conversations. But more than once she said that she was having "a
wonderful party."

And all this occurred in the presence of a miracle. From the moment our mother was brought into the room and saw Mary to the
moment Mary left two hours later, our mother's eyes remained
open in unmistakable amazement, wonder, and joy, as she looked
from one of us to the other in astonishment and gratitude, galvanized, awakened, transfixed, radiantly fulfilled by the sight of her
daughter. The occasion roused her and brought her back from a
kind of sleep that had lasted for years.

11

AT BRIARCLIFF

When I first made the trip by myself to see Mary five years ago, during our mother's final months, I felt as if I might die. I suffer from extreme, if not completely paralyzing, agoraphobia. Any trip along unfamiliar roads is difficult, and the difficulty of this one was compounded with my guilt and anxiety about being Mary's twin, and commingled with the dread my parents used to feel making the same journey. In preparation for making the complete trip, I had had to get used to it, one "leg" at a time, over a period of months. At the same time, the relief of being with Mary once I had gotten there made the effort more than worth it, and in fact made the pain of the journey seem to instantly evaporate as if it had never been there.

Now, after a few tries, I seem to be getting used to this trip. I no longer have to rehearse each section of the road beforehand. Sometimes en route I even forget that I am far from Vermont where I live. Although I still need to stop overnight at a motel along the way, I no longer wake up in the middle of the night there, drenched in sweat, panting heavily from a nightmare.

However, as in all road trips, my soul flounders when I pass through bare countryside, open fields, or uninterrupted woods for any length of time—anywhere where human dwellings are not visible for more than a few miles. If it is a matter of only two or three miles, and I have made the trip previously, noting on one of my yellow pads, "3 miles -0-," for "three miles–empty space," I set my odometer at zero and talk myself through the ensuing moments, trying to relax and monitor the passing increments of road in a dispassionate manner. But if the road is new to me, and I find it taking me deeper into forest or wilderness, a pool of fear starts to rise from my feet upward all the way to my throat, and I start to feel as if I am drowning and have to cry for help. It takes an absurd degree of courage to persevere. In doing research on the problem for my previous book I came upon a bewildering array of possible causes—everything from the purely psychological ("lack of ego support"), to the purely medical ("inner ear disturbances"), to the more generally, if unconvincingly, scientific ("sensitivity to magnetic fields"), to the occult ("effects of previous lives").

The notion of "lack of ego support," while clearly not neurologically specific, does, in its way, ring a bell. Panic does feel like a collapse of whatever armature normally keeps one glued together. In its grip, it is as if nothing were holding "me" ("I" = "Ego" in Latin) up. But why the presence of human habitations, no matter how potentially hostile the residents might in fact be, would constitute a kind of safety net for this collapsing "ego" armature, I can't quite see. I have never been someone who particularly needs "company," and I am often at my happiest left alone to read, work on my music, or even just pay my bills. I find a certain degree of loneliness not only tolerable but deeply pleasurable. Donald Winnicott, the influential pediatrician, psychoanalyst, and author, once wrote a profound, though difficult, essay on the "capacity to be alone," in which, if I understand him correctly, he described comfort in solitude as the result of internalizing the benign watchfulness of parental presences. In other words, when we are contentedly alone, we are able to keep ourselves company. We are both ourselves and our own supportive parent; we know how to draw our own comfort from inside, to draw strength, in fact, from our autonomy. This thought verges on the spiritual, does it not?

By contrast, when I am alone in transition from one place to another, I am easily reduced to a state where I am neither "myself" nor my own "supportive parent."

In trying to grasp the significance this phobia had for me, I reached the rather startling conclusion in my previous thinking and writing that my sister had an enormous amount to do with my problem. I might well have had this type of reaction were I not Mary's twin brother—my father and two of his siblings had similar difficulties—but it most likely would have taken a different form and would have not scared me in the same way that it did. In my case, when I was in a panic state, when the support of the "ego's" rug was ripped out from under me, it felt almost as if I were turning into my sister, as if the unchained spirit of her distress was no longer being held down and was erupting like a monster inside me. Panic reminded me of Mary, the side of me and of my life that I had been making a huge effort—unconsciously, of course—to dispel from my mind. In a sense, panic was my strange way of expressing attachment.

As I started to pay close attention to my own reactions on the road, for example—during the period when I was working on my book on phobias I was scribbling not only mileage and landmarks to remember on my yellow pads while I drove but also thoughts and impressions—I noticed that I was sometimes even more disturbed by abandoned houses or, worse, abandoned *groups* of houses—ghost towns—than by woods and fields. Passing houses that looked as if they hadn't been painted in a generation or two, or were mostly boarded up, or where there had been a fire and an old rusty truck with one tire removed lay at a tilt in the driveway, created a fierce mental dissonance in me. *Is there someone there or not?* Such areas replicated the creepiness of the dream of the old man in Bergman's *Wild Strawberries*: clocks without hands; a carriage without a driver; a figure standing at the end of the street who turns out to be just an empty sack.

Somehow, for me, the open road released the pain inherent in the tantalizing sense that Mary was fully alive but, in significant respects, absent from the human conversation, or at least the human conversation I could participate in. This is a pain I do not feel at all when I am with her. But in the presence of mute mountains and trees or, most of all, houses that may or may not contain human beings—life that is animate but mute and incomprehensible—I feel the presence of my fears about what lies behind Mary's penetrating gaze, about who she is, as if she herself embodies the age-old questions about what part of us is matter, what part soul; the terror that we are only matter and are only imagining that we have souls. The houses where humanity may or may not reside replicate the uncanny feeling one can have with those who suffer from Alzheimer's disease or dementia or other kinds of mental impairment, who appear so completely of this world yet don't see what we see, and speak, if they do, from a place we don't recognize.

Of course I wasn't carrying only these things with me on the road. I was most of all carrying the burden of the decision my parents had made all those years ago, one I am sure they agonized over and continued to agonize over ever after, to send their child to live away from the family. I carried their agony with me and I carried their guilt, and I felt both their guilt and my own guilt at having been "spared." I could feel a strange psychological pressure inside me. It was the kind of paradoxical emotion one has when a lover who has been nasty suddenly turns affectionate, and instead of welcoming the affection—which is exactly what one has been longing for—one rebuffs her. Then, having acted exactly in the opposite way of one's desires, one is left to feel a sense of crushing defeat and a terrible loneliness. As if demonstrating an equation from a law of physics, my desire to reach Mary's new home was canceled by dread, a dread equal to the pain of our original separation.

Being unable to articulate feelings is hardly evidence that we lack them. In accounts of autistic children being sent to school for the first time there are a few in which the parents are surprised by their child's sudden expression of grief at separation. Did Mary experience feelings of heartsickness and abandonment when she was eight years old? Having now grieved for both my parents, I can speak firsthand about the biological nature of such feelings—how they happen to you, as much as in you. They descend upon your body, no matter what you are thinking, or think you are "feeling." They happen as surely as the trembling that happens when you are in mortal danger. We don't know about Mary's "feelings," but we can guess what they might be from those we ourselves have that are beyond reasoning, or conceptualizing, or words. Surely there is more than a "need for sameness" in the happy look on Mary's face when she sees her family members.

When one is en route from one place to another, one's emotions are somehow set loose, like birds let out of a cage and then out the window. The windows open, and our emotions fly up and out. We can almost hear them saying, "Finally! You let me out! We're free!" Sometimes the emotions are joyful—a sense of infinite possibilities opening up—sometimes the opposite.

What was this pain I felt on the road in dense fog, or when the countryside opened up to reveal vistas of shrubbery or groves of trees charred by fire, or on winding dirt roads lined with foliage obscuring the view—in short, whenever I was isolated, whenever there was no way to orient myself in relation to other people?

I try to remember, but all I can feel is that there is something in the past—a blank space—that is just too terrible to think about, and that there are no words for it.

The blank space of imagining what Mary felt when she was left at Chatham and then when she was driven to her new home in Delaware, or imagining what she felt when her parents and brothers appeared for two hours, had lunch, and then left again.

The blank space in my mother when she drove away, leaving her daughter behind.

The pain of trying to reach her in the car, and the pain of her permanent inaccessibility, even when I have arrived and am there with her.

Something too terrible, for which there are no words: Is it a trauma? Is it actually something, or is it not more like "nothing"? An infant sends out his radar, as he discovers how to look, as he discovers what is "out there," what is inside and what is "outside," without having words, or ideas that are more than shadows in the mind; as he discovers what is "me" and what is "you"; as he forms habits of doing, and finds reactions "out there," eventually even confirmation—without a word for that—that certain things happen a certain way, eventually even that certain things he does cause certain reactions. An infant learns by bouncing his cries, his gestures, his impulses, against things and people—people who may be strangers, parents, siblings, or a twin, of course. What if this bouncing occurs in a vacuum that has no name, which is never confirmed as one? What if these first assertions are received by a kind of blankness? What if the space he enters when he is with his first and original companion in the world requires him at all times to abandon any hope of having his self confirmed?

I get out of the car. I have left word that I will meet Mary in what is called the "vocational" facility, the place she spends part of each weekday morning and afternoon doing a rudimentary job, for which she is then paid in an account that she can draw from. I am admitted through a metal door by some strong-looking fellows who seem almost twice my size. As I walk down the hallway and hear the busy din from the workroom, I am somehow reminded of my trips to visit Bridgewater Prison as a volunteer teacher when I was eighteen and at Harvard. I recognize the feeling of entering an enclosed world that is set apart, and I realize for the first time that I had sought out that experience long ago just at the time that Mary herself entered this very place.

When I enter the cavernous space where groups of men and women are seated at tables performing their tasks, I feel enveloped in a faintly festive atmosphere. Rightly or wrongly one senses an air of camaraderie and industriousness. As I adjust to the space and to the strangeness of many of the people there, I see that everyone is seated at long tables placing materials in boxes or affixing labels on objects that are being wrapped. Men and women form separate groups, often at adjoining tables. Everyone's place is marked with a label on the table itself. Clearly they are there every day. A friendly Chinese woman points me toward the other end of the hall.

Mary sees me almost immediately and comes to get me. She is wearing her thick glasses, which sparkle opaquely over her smile. She has a strange hopping, slightly lopsided way of walking, tilting a bit to one side. She grabs my hand in her characteristic way and brings me over to her table. She looks happy. A small woman with a tight face and highly mobile features—her name is Juanita, I see from her name tag—gestures meaningfully and points to a chair, making a strange sound as if her mouth is covered. Her eyes pinch together; she looks concerned about me. Later I learn that she is mute. I sit where she has suggested, next to my sister.

There are perhaps ten other women around the table, two of whom are employees of the institution. One is an exceptionally beautiful young black woman, Cicely, who is in a late stage of pregnancy. I ask her when she is due, and in a gentle African accent she says in six weeks.

The room is noisy and without adornment of any kind—at best one would call it nondescript—but the atmosphere is purposeful and cheerful. I soon realize that the groups around each table come from the different units at the campus, and that the women around the table are Mary's housemates. Along with Juanita, there is a woman named Sarah who maintains a quiet, wistful smile at all times and gives very little sign of noticing what is happening around her. Her eyes look at me but seem not to register me. She has lovely, tranquil features, but it is as if a heavy weight were bearing down on the top of her head, keeping it in an absolutely fixed, stationary position. Yet when I mention her name to Mary, her smile deepens and widens. There is also Dawn, whose face is drawn and hatchet-shaped, with very sunken eyes. When she gets up from the table I see that although she has a normal torso, she has a gigantic trunk and bottom and extraordinarily thick, heavy legs. From time to time many of the ladies get up and stroll around. At several points during the next hour some of the men clients come over to Cicely and either give her a hug, joke with her, or gently pat her swollen belly, which she graciously accepts.

In the middle of the long table is a stack of boxes containing umbrellas that need to be relabeled. Cicely opens the boxes and hands each woman a pile of umbrellas. They each have piles of adhesive stickers next to them. Mary's attention is riveted on her job, carefully removing the plastic cover of each umbrella, placing a new bar-coded sticker over the old one, and then replacing the plastic. (The label says "100% Nylon.") She does this over and over, and while she is one of the fastest, she is also steady and careful. Every once in a while she holds up the umbrella and seems to be proudly evaluating it, like a carpenter standing back from his handiwork. Not for the first time I notice her strong resemblance to my father.

Every twenty minutes or so a buzzer sounds and a voice comes over the intercom announcing a new shift in the dining hall down the corridor. Toward 11:30 I notice that the women seem to know that it will soon be time to go to lunch. They are putting the umbrellas in piles and not asking for new ones. When the voice speaks through the intercom at 11:30 our group lines up to go to the cafeteria, which is just down the hall in the same compound. Others remain at their tables working. I gather that the units eat in shifts. Mary asks me if I have brought her the Reese's Peanut Butter Cups she always expects. I say that I have them with me in the car. She takes my hand again and leads me to the cafeteria with seriousness and a sense of the habitual. The room is somewhat smaller than the factorylike hall we just left, more like an elementary school lunchroom, painted a light beige, with long tables in rows, seating perhaps a hundred, and in it the behavior of the clients is noticeably more rowdy. We are served meatball sandwiches, which we take on trays to the table at the farthest end of the room. Mary asks me if I would buy her a Coke from the Coke machine, which I do. This is not a habitual drink and is in fact a rare treat. At first I am not sure that I can distinguish between the clients and the caretakers, but after a few moments it becomes clear. Every once in a while I receive a polite nod of greeting from a member of the staff. A young man in his early twenties—clearly a "client"—passes by me several times in a row and says, "Hi, Chief!" each time.

I am seated next to Mary and we are eating our sandwiches. Around us there is an almost zoolike atmosphere. In the vocational unit everyone was focused on a common task and behaved in a relatively uniform manner, while here it is as if a flood of varied behaviors has been released, often accompanied by wild vocalizing. Although the ages of the people in the room range from twenty to eighty, it feels like an elementary school at recess. But in contrast to an elementary school, while there is motion and commotion and sound, surprisingly little of it represents interaction between people. When there are true exchanges taking place, the bulk of them seem to be between staff and clients. Otherwise there is mostly concentration on eating.

However, there are also some clients who are as outgoing as talkative youngsters. A youngish man, outrageously friendly, introduces me to a burly aide, patting him affectionately on the back and telling me, "He's a good guy. He's a good guy. He's a good guy.

Strong like you." (He is my physical opposite.) "Do you like him? Do you like him?" He comes by more than once pointing out the aide, who is strong-looking but actually quite shy, repeating these compliments and questions each time. Finally he urges us to wave to each other, which we do.

At a distance I see a group of clients in very animated, exhilarated conversation with a member of the staff, hanging on to each other and laughing, apparently telling her a story, looking for her approval and signs of shared amusement.

Mary asks me again about the Reese's Peanut Butter Cups. Her question is in the form of an assertion with a tone of worry attached to it: "AllenbroughtReese'sPeanutButterCups—?" I reassure her. She then gets up since she also has a job here in the cafeteria, receiving the trays from each client and emptying their dishes onto the rubberized conveyer belt leading to the kitchen. As I remain at our table, Mary puts on an apron, plastic gloves, and headgear that looks like a transparent shower cap and goes to stand by the garbage can to receive the trays. The buzzer sounds and the intercom announces the next influx of customers, who file in energetically. Everyone else leaves, handing their trays to Mary and her colleague, a tall man who wears an apron and a string tied tightly around his head. I look more closely to see if the string is actually part of some kind of hair net, and it is not. It looks like something he feels compelled to wear.

Around me the seats fill with new faces, all eating, many with unusual habits. The clients who are physically unable to feed themselves are being helped by aides, who put large plastic bibs around them. The face of one young man has eyes that are heavily bandaged by sheer strips; another has raw, bloody wounds on his forehead and cheeks. Some from this group are in wheelchairs. A woman with cerebral palsy is being fitted with a bib, then fed. A young man is wearing an odd-looking protective helmet, through which he is drinking from a straw. A blind Asian boy with an elongated, strangely beautiful face is being fed by another lovely African American woman. She is quite dressed up in a colorful blouse and skirt, and has red and orange tints in her hair. An aide comes by to cut the food of a large, sluggish-looking man at my side. I am astonished to look down only moments later to see that the man has almost instantly polished off every bite.

There is a great deal of action but less interaction. There is an argument at the next table, but it may be between aides. Most people seem to be in their own worlds. A boy near me talks covertly into his left hand after every bite, as if into a walkie-talkie. It seems to be a part of his eating ritual. He speaks the words with great rapidity and clarity, but they are indecipherable. In the distance, Mary looks serious and focused and very responsible clearing trays. Whenever there is a break she comes down to where I am sitting and asks again about the Reese's Peanut Butter Cups. There is an amazing sense of familiarity between us. She doesn't show the slightest uneasiness or surprise about the fact that once again I am in her vicinity. I have the impression she is pleased to show me what her routine is, and is not self-conscious about it. Every twenty or twenty-five minutes, the intercom sounds and there are new arrivals, and more tray-clearing.

An innocent-looking young woman faces my way at the next table. Having finished eating, she is staring meaningfully into the middle distance with a half-smile, as if secretly pleased by something. She looks like a fresh-faced divinity student, intelligent, thoughtful. After twenty minutes she starts to rock back and forth. A woman at the other side of the table slaps the back of her head repeatedly and audibly every minute or so, exactly where she is in fact completely bald. She eventually stands up and, as if obeying an inner command, starts to rock back and forth, like someone davening at temple. Another youngish man is rocking while twisting his arms and entwining his hands around the opposite elbows. A boy not far from me repeatedly tells an aide that he is "disgusted" by his meatball sandwich and won't finish it. Several clients remind me of friends of mine. One resembles a distinguished composer I know, but has a strange grin that gives him a slightly diabolical look. Another, who has steadily rocked back and forth since arriving at the lunch table, looks like a former schoolmate of mine who became a doctor. An extremely short woman bringing her tray to Mary with a jovial expression on her face may in fact be a man: she has long dark hair and pronounced facial hair, tiny feet, and wears thick glasses; she appears to be wearing a bra beneath a nearly transparent shirt.

Eventually we go back in the now familiar vocational center to work on the umbrellas. When the workday ends, the women are driven back to Mary's "unit" to have snacks. While we drink iced water in cups from a cooler in the dining area, Mary finally gets to enjoy the Reese's Peanut Butter Cups, which she eats with no concern for the fact that they have partially melted. The evening schedule lists swimming in the late afternoon followed by dinner and movies from 6 to 9 p.m.

My head is spinning from the impressions of the afternoon. Just by sitting in the cafeteria for a few hours I grew gradually accustomed to a kind of expanded sense of the human spectrum. I was reminded of the experiences I have had hearing quarter-tone music. At first it sounds out of tune because one listens to it with ears accustomed to music in which the octave is divided into twelve half steps, instead of the twenty-four gradations present in quarter-tone music. But after a while it begins to sound right and like a different way of being "in tune." Afterward, in fact, half steps by comparison seem large.

Mary and I sit together on a sofa in a side room, and I show her some family photos I have brought with me. I have been worried about showing her photos of our parents, now that they are both dead. Mary learned the news of our father's death back in 1992 from her trusted psychologist, Anna, a woman who fortunately has an extraordinary ability to communicate with her clients in a direct, affectionate, and respectful way. In 2005 I had asked Anna to be with me and help me communicate that our mother had died. Anna used the phrase that Mary associates with death, saying that both our mother and father were now "in heaven," and Mary had understood that this meant that she would not be seeing them again. Nevertheless, sometimes she would seem to forget and include their names in her list of who was coming to visit her, and she would need to be reminded. Mary does not seem to ever cry out of sadness, but that does not necessarily mean that she doesn't ever feel sad. During one of our hotel lunches with her after our father's death I said to her that I missed "having Daddy at the table." She looked me with her most serious expression and put her hand on my arm, saying, "Missdaddyatthetable."

As so often happens, she does what she is asked to do, looking at each photograph when I hand it to her, and when asked, identifying whomever she recognizes. The pictures are arranged in no particular order, and some date back to when she was five years old. She instantly recognizes a picture of Bessie taken in the early 1950s. She frequently recognizes our brother. She has some uncertainty about our father. She knows me immediately at most ages, even at the age of eight, but seeing a few of the photos of me when I am older, she refers to me as "Daddy." When it comes to recognizing her mother at any age, she is never wrong. Even when I show her a picture of our young mother taken in 1948, the year of our birth, sporting an unfamiliar hairstyle of luxurious long black hair and bangs, she says with great energy, "I think Mommy." I can't recall ever hearing her use the expression "I think."

I remind her that I am hoping to do another of our birthday lunches in Vermont as we did last summer for the first time on our sixtieth birthday. Mary was brought up for the morning, I remind her, and she got to see Annie and Harold; my wife, Yoshiko; and our little infant son, Noa, who was then only six weeks old. We had chicken salad, ice cream, and cake. This time our brother can be there, I say. "Wallace, Mary, Allen . . . ," she says.

I have never spent as much time with Mary as I have today. No—that it isn't true. Before the age of eight, we spent many whole days together. And before the age of three, we were rarely apart. And much earlier, when no one could see us at all, or knew that there were two of us, we were together, and only together.

I can see that she is getting tired. Finally I tell her I need to leave, and she says, "Allen will see you soon," and I say, "I'll be back in the winter," and she says, "Allenwillseeyouinthewinter." I give her a hug and say, "I love you, Mary," get in the car, and drive off.

As always, driving releases emotions in me. Out of nowhere, I start to cry. I see a vision of life as a spiral staircase that one ascends through darkness interspersed with pools of light, never knowing how long the staircase is, or whether it is dark or light at the top. I see my father's face, and he is crying. Not for the first time, I think back to the tiny impromptu ceremony six of us had standing next to my mother's coffin, and I remember the sound of Piergiorgio's

voice as he recited these lines in Italian, from a poem by Salvatore
Quasimodo:

> Ognuno sta solo sul cuor della terra
> Trafitto da un raggio di sole:
> Ed è subito sera.

> *Everyone stands alone on the heart of the earth*
> *Transfixed by a sun-ray:*
> *And suddenly it is evening.*

ACKNOWLEDGMENTS

I want to acknowledge the following books, articles, and videos, which provided me with an indispensable grounding in the scientific and human dimensions of my subject when I was preparing to write this book. I have quoted from most of these sources in the text.

On the subject of autism spectrum disorders, I want to make special mention of the book *Autism and Asperger Syndrome*, edited by Uta Frith, which includes Hans Asperger's paper "'Autistic Psychopathy' in Childhood," first published in *Archiv für Psychiatrie und Nervenkrankheiten* in 1944; Frith's *Autism: Explaining the Enigma*; the article "Autistic Disturbances of Affective Contact," by Leo Kanner, in *Nervous Child* 2 (1943); *The Wild Boy of Aveyron*, by Jean Itard; *Thinking in Pictures* and *Emergence: Labeled Autistic*, both by Temple Grandin; *A Real Person*, by Gunilla Gerland; the article "Light and Number: Ordering Principles in the World of an Autistic Child," by David Park and Philip Youderian, in the *Journal of Autism and Childhood Schizophrenia* 4, no. 4 (1974); and

"Adult Recollections of a Formerly Autistic Child," by Jules R. Bemorad, in *Journal of Autism and Developmental Disorders* 9, no. 2 (1979).

I also benefited enormously from reading *Autism and Asperger Syndrome: The Facts* and *Mindblindness: An Essay on Autism and Theory of Mind*, both by Simon Baron-Cohen; *Autism: The Facts*, by Simon Baron-Cohen and Patrick Bolton; *Autism in History: The Case of Hugh Blair of Borgue*, by Rab Houston and Uta Frith; the article "Advances in Autism Genetics: On the Threshold of a New Neurobiology," by Brett S. Abrahams and Daniel H. Geschwind, in *Nature Reviews Genetics* (May 2008); and *Unstrange Minds*, by Roy Richard Grinker; as well as from viewing the Oliver Sacks video "Rage for Order: Autism," from the 1998 BBC series *The Mind Traveller*; and the interview of Temple Grandin, "Stairway to Heaven," in the televised documentary series *Errol Morris' First Person*.

In researching the work of psychologist Bruno Bettelheim, I viewed two BBC documentaries on Bettelheim, *Bruno Bettelheim: A Sense of Surviving* and *Bruno Bettelheim: The Man Who Cared for Children*; and consulted *Rising to the Light: A Portrait of Bruno Bettelheim*, by Theron Raines; *The Creation of Dr. B: A Biography of Bruno Bettelheim*, by Richard Pollak; as well as Bettelheim's own writings: *Surviving and Other Essays, Love Is Not Enough, Freud's Vienna and Other Essays, Truants from Life*, and *The Empty Fortress*.

Although there are a number of books dealing with the phenomenon of twin loss, the three books that I found most helpful in writing about being a twin were general in nature: *Twins: From Fetus to Child* and *Twins in the World*, both by Alessandra Piontelli; and *Entwined Lives*, by Nancy Segal.

I also greatly benefited from reading the book *A Healing Family*, by the Japanese novelist Kenzaburo Oe.

Many individuals aided me in my work on this book, most especially a few whose names I cannot divulge. I owe those in this group a particular debt of gratitude. I also wish to particularly thank my brother, Wallace Shawn, for his indispensable help and support, as well as my dear wife, Yoshiko Sato; our little son, Noa; and my two grown-up children, Annie Shawn and Harold Shawn, for theirs. I am also deeply indebted to Dr. Alexander Westphal and Dr. Abha R. Gupta for offering their valuable expert perspectives on autism spectrum disorders; to Betsy Blachly for her thoughts on the treatment of children with autism; to Dr. Marriane Makman for her memories of her mother, Herta Wertheim; and to Dr. Marjorie LaRowe for her invaluable advice and insights. In addition, I want to express my gratitude to the following friends, colleagues, and experts in the mental health and related fields, who gave generously of their time, expertise, and ideas in discussions I had with them while preparing this book: Hank Chapin, Edith Iglauer Daly, Dr. Jayne Danien, Anda Durso, Jay Hamburger, Michelle Hogle, Dr. Mark Reber, Dr. Stephen Reibel, and my Bennington College colleagues ("Drs." all), Ronald Cohen, Eileen Scully, Elizabeth (Betsy) Sherman, Bruce Weber, and Kerry Woods. I also want to extend my deepest thanks to Maria Astorga, Marina Barnett, Isabel Fox, Marjorie Graham, Aimée Guerin, Thomas Hayes, Deborah Mills Hayes, Amy Hoch, Piergiorgio Nicoletti, Dorothy Rubel, Frederick Seidel, Dr. Frederick Stern, Rebekah Westphal, Kathy Williams, and Oceana Wilson. Finally I wish to humbly thank Lynn Nesbit, my literary agent, for her kindness and helpfulness, and extend my deepest gratitude to my editors, Wendy Wolf and Margaret Riggs, for their graciousness, brilliance, skill, and understanding.

INDEX